UNDERSTANDING THE STRATEGIES OF SATAN

Samou

Kingdom Publishers

Understanding the Strategies of Satan
Preparing Humanity for Eternity
Copyright© Samuel Foday Koroma

All rights reserved. No part of this book may be reproduced in any form by photocopying or any electronic or mechanical means, including information storage or retrieval systems, without permission in writing from both the copyright owner and the publisher of the book. The right of Samou to be identified as the author of this work has been asserted by him in accordance with the Copyright, Designs and Patents Act 1988 and any subsequent amendments thereto. A catalogue record for this book is available from the British Library.

All Scripture Quotations have been taken from the King James Version of the Bible.

ISBN: 978-1-911697-14-5

1st Edition by Kingdom Publishers

Kingdom Publishers
London, UK.

You can purchase copies of this book from any leading bookstore or email **contact@kingdompublishers.co.uk**

Dedication

This book is dedicated to all Christians. I pray that as you read, the Holy Spirit would enhance your understanding - in the Name of Jesus Christ.

Contents

Acknowledgement	9
Preface	11
Chapter 1 : The Spirit of Unbelief	13
Chapter 2 : The Will	27
Chapter 3 : The Power of Fornication	38
Chapter 4 : Demonic Control	54
Chapter 5 : Contaminated Doctrine	64
Chapter 6 : The 'Judge Not' Slogan	72
Chapter 7 : Phoney Prophets	82
Chapter 8 : The Sunday Service	95
Chapter 9 : Divine Acronyms	106
Chapter 10 : The Chocolate Gospel	113
Chapter 11 : The Spirit of Unforgiveness	127
Chapter 12 : Slandering	141
Chapter 13 : The Reality of Hell	148
Chapter 14 : The End-Time Army	157
Chapter 15 : Get Ready	173
Addendum	186

Acknowledgement

Be sober, be vigilant; because your adversary the devil, as a roaring lion, walketh about, seeking whom he may devour - 1 Peter 5:8.

I congratulate our heavenly Father, His son Jesus and the Holy Spirit for using me as a vessel to unveil the strategies of Satan to humanity. Writing this holy revelation was a tough spiritual battle, but when you work with Jesus, victory remains a lifestyle.

Preface

'And there was war in heaven: Michael and his angels fought against the dragon; and the dragon fought and his angels, And prevailed not; neither was their place found any more in heaven. And the great dragon was cast out, that old serpent, called the Devil, and Satan, which deceiveth the whole world: he was cast out into the earth, and his angels were cast out with him' – Revelation 12:7-9.

The battle for human souls began when Lucifer and Satan was kicked out of heaven, as a result of rebelling against the Almighty God. Satan was able to cajole a limited fraction of the angels of heaven to join his devilish campaign. But as expected, he lost the battle to the loyal hosts of heaven. And together with his fellow angelic rebels, the demons, he was kicked out of the Almighty God's holy habitat and into the earth. Satan knows his time is short, so as we get closer to the Rapture Phase, he strives to help throw as many humans as he can into the eternal demonic domain. But he does that in so many ways which might be hidden to humanity.

Satan's major attack is against Christians – against the Church. If he could paralyse the body of Christ – God Forbid, then the world would safely sail into his kingdom because humanity would be nakedly defenceless. As a Christian, you must be aware that the Church is in combat with the army of Satan. But our Lord Jesus has established an end-time army and is continually raising Christian soldiers to pull down the strongholds of Satan. Already, we know our weapon, the name of Jesus, is more powerful than that of the devil. We know we are more equipped than Satan and his dark angels. We know we're stronger than the devil and his demons. But when soldiers go to war, they plan before advancing. And during that planning phase, they need to understand the tricks and strengths of the 'enemy', without which fighting would be difficult and their lives would remain in jeopardy. If we, Christians, do not understand Satan's strategies, we might run into an ambush and suffer undeserved defeat. We must understand his methodologies, which would establish us on a good platform to face and overcome his army.

Generally, Satan uses sin to keep humanity under his control. So whatever he does, he does it to run man into sin. Yes, some of his ways are easily detected. But he works in so many other ways that can only be uncovered with the help of the Holy Spirit. Some of those satanic ways are hidden, even to many Christians. But our Lord Jesus is preparing Christians for His coming, as He wants to receive His bride, the Church, without blemish – Ephesians 5:27. **Understanding the Strategies of Satan** deals with real-time situations. It's not mainly centred on how demons operate in the underworld and other satanic realms. Rather, it uncovers human occurrences, in everyday life, that Satan uses to entrap humanity. Satan fights to keep Unbelievers caged in his dark world; he fights to steal the salvation of Christians and isolate man from his assignment – to distort your earthly path. His major goal is to permanently separate man from the Almighty God. But when you understand Satan's strategies, you will be able to recognise his demonic traps; you will be able to escape them and establish a healthy relationship with your Maker.

Eternity is full of surprises. Many Christians, who believe they're qualified for heaven, get rejected by our Lord Jesus when they face Him on judgement. To many who were seen as spiritual giants in the Church, Jesus says, 'Depart from me'. Some who're not even considered in the body of Christ receive crowns of dignity. Why? There're strategies of Satan Christians need to understand. **Understanding the Strategies of Satan** helps prepare Christians for the second coming of our Lord Jesus. But even if you depart the earth before Christ's arrival, you will be able to save a safe place in heaven. This book walks Unbelievers into the kingdom of the Almighty God, as well. So I strongly advise you remain intensely prayerful, as we expose that old serpent to every character. He's going to be fierce and would fight back. But we're untouchable, as we're highly protected by our heavenly defensive weapon – the name of Jesus – Proverbs 18:10.

Chapter I

The Spirit of Unbelief

Demonic hazes continuously hover around humanity, as inhabitants grapple for planetary survival. The drum of an emerging life-seizure begins to sound. The atmosphere keeps mutating and the smart would begin to decipher the fragrance of eternal celebration. The devil fights to institute a demonic blockage, and establish his real-time deprivation of heavenly possession. Cunningly, he befriends the ignorant, in surprised expectation of a gloomy future. Roaring to embrace defiant broods, a holy generation ever succeeds to undermine the dark tries of the dragon. And untiringly, Satan employs multiple strategies to eternally separate human creatures from their Creator. The objective of that old serpent is to get humanity to ignore the source of their immortality. Satan desires to see man disobey the Almighty God. He aims to get man to obey his detrimental protocols. But he does that in so many ways, some of which can only be revealed by the spirit of our eternal Father. As a Christian, you must truly understand Satan's tricks to successfully execute your assignment and maintain your salvation in this physical domain.

In the garden of Eden, the Almighty God instructed man to eat of any other tree, but not of the tree of knowledge of good and evil. He cautioned that the day man feeds from it, man shall surely die – Genesis 2:16-17. And in verses 1-6 of chapter 3 of the same book of Genesis, man was deceived by that old serpent, who emphasized that the Almighty God instructed man to not eat of that tree because man's eyes would be opened and recognise good and evil. And indeed, the Almighty God did reveal in Genesis 3:22 that man detected good and evil, after suckling from the tree. Satan, many times, presents camouflaged packages that seem right to man, but the end produces eternal devastation. The deception man accommodated from the devil led to a divine separation between man and the Almighty God. But even with man's disobedience, God loves man so much and would do all to bring back His lost creation. Satan says man would not die if man eats from the tree, which implies man should not believe what the Almighty God warns of. Satan sets man against his Maker. And when man is wrapped up in unbelief, relating with his heavenly Father triggers another phase of spiritual warfare.

Satan infiltrates the Church. He walks into the body of Christ unidentified and many Christians do not detect many of his strategies. The numerous denominational applications of Christianity depict that the spirit of unbelief operates even amid people who believe they are true followers of Jesus Christ. Some believe Jesus is the Son of God but denies He is God. Some proclaim they believe in the Trinity, but deprecate the operations of the Holy Spirit. Some accept demons can still be cast out today, whilst others reject. Others believe anointed servants of God can raise the dead today, whilst others see it as a make-up. Some believe in tongues and interpretation of tongues, but others tag it a divine mockery. How can people who all claim to be followers of Jesus Christ believe differently about Jesus? There is only one Holy Spirit who teaches man about Jesus. The trouble is that some do not understand His teachings, others do not adhere to His teachings, and some do not even have a relationship with the Holy Spirit. The Holy Bible which guides Christians is not like the mathematical text we used in our schools. It's not like the biological course we're taught in schools. The Bible is a spiritual book, inspired by God, so you need the spirit of the Almighty God to help you understand. At schools, when students are equally taught on a specific subject, they emerge with different grades, on examination. Why? This is majorly due to disparities in talents and intelligence quotient levels. The Almighty God is the most brilliant personality with an immeasurable level of intelligence. He knew if He left humanity to read and understand the Holy Scriptures all by themselves, there would be discrepancies, as in school examinations. That's one of the reasons He sent the Holy Spirit - to teach us. If we all allow and apply the counselling of the Holy Spirit, the Church would speak with one voice. Christianity would operate in unanimity. But in many cases, the teachings some receive are contaminated by Satan and their insensitivity cultivates difficulty to discern erroneous doctrines. Believing, and accepting Jesus for who He truly is remains a function of how much you understand of Him. Jesus deeply cares about whether your belief is right or wrong, as He only sees a Believer or an Unbeliever. Some are Protestants. Others are Anglicans. Some belong to the Roman Catholic. Some say they're the Latter-Day Saints. Others call themselves Jehovah's Witnesses. Some others make choices of being Scientologists. They all interpret the Scriptures as they understand. The trouble with denominational practices is that they influence your belief and you might run onto the wrong path. If you belong to a group with contaminated belief, then Jesus considers you an Unbeliever. Whether you're 80% correct and 20% wrong, it doesn't count. You cannot believe in Jesus partially. You cannot believe He has the power to raise the dead and denies He is the Son of God. You cannot believe He is the Son of God and do not believe He is God. How can you believe in the Trinity, but do not believe in the operations of the Holy Spirit? How can you believe in the operations of the Holy Spirit and oppose the heavenly tongues? When the disciples of Jesus assembled on the day of Pentecost, praying with one accord, a strong wind enveloped them – they were filled with the Holy Ghost and began to speak in diverse tongues, to an extent that even Unbelievers were amazed at hearing them speak their languages – Acts 2:1-8. Jesus cares about what you believe of Him. Do you believe He is the Son of God? Do you believe He is God? Do you believe He died and resurrected? It's the resurrection power of Jesus that empowers Christians. And if your answers to those questions are 'No', or at least a 'No', then you need to pray for the Almighty God to help your unbelief.

True understanding of our Lord Jesus shows up in many ways. But two of the majors include the Holy Bible and direct revelation from Him. But either way, it must be empowered by the Holy Spirit or else you get deceived by Satan. The Scripture advises meditating on the holy book day and night – Joshua 1:8. The Bible should be your good friend. You need to study your Bible daily. Like your school textbooks; the more you read it, the more you become familiar with the Scriptures. And as you depend on the Holy Spirit, the more you understand. From personal experience, reading the Bible might seem boring, especially for a start. When you pick up worldly novels, you get more enthusiastic as you read. They become intriguing and you wouldn't want to accommodate even a second of unrelated distraction. But as you unfold the pages of a Bible or any other form of ecclesiastical writing, you feel sleepy. You begin to yawn. That's a trick of Satan to interrupt your desired belief. Satan knows when you continue ingesting the holy spiritual victuals, the truth about the Almighty God would be revealed to you. You need to keep reading and would realize how exciting the Word of God is. The bible supports life. The Word of God energizes your spirit and soul. The Holy Bible is not like other worldly books. It was written by holy men, inspired by the Almighty God. Apostle Paul, who wrote many books in the New Testament, was a man persecuting Christians. But he had a personal encounter with our Lord Jesus, which transformed the rest of his life path. During his ministry, he was ever ready to separate his soul from his body for the gospel of our Lord Jesus Christ. John, who wrote the Book of Revelation, was an intimate disciple of our Lord Jesus. John physically walked with Jesus, ate with Him, and prayed with Him when He lived on earth. The Bible is the Christian constitution – the Christian guide. It's full of power. Remember, life is about the spiritual and physical. As you feed your physical body, you need to feed your spirit-man – you need to 'eat' the word of God. By that, your belief reinforces and you spiritually grow. Many might not understand that 'belief' grows. The Bible talks about 'Faith as a grain of mustard seed' – Matthew 17:20. It's a small seed, which grows into a huge tree. With that kind of faith, you would do great miracles – in the name of Jesus. That implies there are different levels of faith. Synonymously, there are different levels of belief. As a baby Christian, your belief will be minute. But as you become stronger in the word, your belief grows and your bond with our Lord Jesus becomes more fortified. By the way, a baby Christian is not defined as a new convert. A baby Christian is a follower of Jesus Christ who is not truly matured in the Christian principles. You can be in the ministry for fifty years and still be a baby Christian. Someone who got saved a year ago can be spiritually matured. However, a baby Christian can be a new convert, but not in all cases. I find it amusing when some Christians position a Bible underneath their pillows, especially when sleeping to protect themselves from demons and other satanic agents. That's a myth! You can hide ten Bibles underneath your pillow, if your belief speaks in opposition to the instructions of our Lord Jesus, a single demon can separate your perceived protection into particles. It's your belief that connects you to our Lord Jesus. And you have to remain careful, as the same Bible you study to gain spiritual maturity can become an idol and work against you. The Bible is full of power. But the power is in the written word of God, not on the pages or the cover. So the Bible only becomes powerful to you, when you understand and apply the written words. To increase your knowledge of the Word of God, you need not only read the Holy Bible. There are inspiring Christian books, written by anointed Christians, which analyse the Word of God. You can also read Christian articles, listen to Christian preachers in-person — live or on audio and video recordings. The Holy Spirit helps us understand His word. But there are spiritual gifts offered to different Christians. Some have the Gift of Knowledge, whilst others have the Gift of Mercy. Some have the Gift of Prophecy. The Scripture reveals that if you have faith as a mustard seed, you would say to this mountain, 'Be thou removed, and be thou cast into the sea', and it shall be done. This is applicable by all Christians, in every situation. But, as I mentioned, there are spiritual gifts and some are gifted to carry out miracles. Some Christians are anointed to do signs and wonders — these would do mighty miracles more than other Christians. Similarly, regarding understanding the Word of God, some Christians are gifted with the spirit of wisdom. Some are gifted with the spirit of knowledge. They understand the Word of God more than others and can even teach them. So you do not only depend on your understanding, but need to work with others, as well. You need to gain from the wisdom and knowledge of other Christians.

You can get more knowledge of Jesus through a personal encounter with Him. Jesus appears to His chosen ones at chosen times. He appears in any form, as He pleases. Jesus can appear to man, physically. He can appear in a vision. He can appear to man through dreams. He can appear in whatever way He desires. Generally, Jesus appears to man to reveal information on what has happened, what's happening and what is to happen, including divine instructions. Secondly, Jesus appears to reveal His true identity to man. In His revelation to John, Jesus unfolds messages about creation: in the past, about current existence and about what would happen as we approach the end of the world. Jesus also reveals His true identity when he says, 'I AM ALPHA and OMEGA – the BEGINNING and END; the FIRST and the LAST '– Revelation 1:8. Jesus always appears on assignment. He does not appear to some individuals directly. He appears to other Christians and expects them to reveal the outcome of their encounter – Matthew 10:27. By that, He teaches humanity the principle of faith. You don't need to see before believing. He teaches Christians to develop faith. He teaches man to believe, without which your relation with Him would remain deformed. Jesus gives some the gift of prophecy or revelation. Such Christians see and speak the mind of God. They relay information from God to man. But all forms of revelation must be driven by the Holy Spirit – John 16:13. The purpose of the gospel is to unify humanity and bring unbelievers back into the hands of our Lord Jesus, but how can that goal be achieved when Christians are divided in beliefs? Satan establishes and promotes division through unbelief. There is no room for partial belief in Christianity. However, as I stated earlier, your belief can begin small and with the help of the Holy Spirit, grow. But you must get to the point of total belief. You either totally believe or you don't believe at all. You cannot believe in the holy Scriptures partially. The same God who inspired the Old Testament is the same God who inspired the New Testament. The same God who inspired the writing of the Book of Genesis is the same God who inspired the writing of the Book of Revelation.

Isaiah prophesied about the eternal sovereignty of our Lord Jesus, even before His physical revelation on earth. In his divine message, Prophet Isaiah says, ' For unto us a child is born, unto us a son is given: and the government shall be upon his shoulder: and His name shall be called Wonderful, Counsellor, the mighty God, the everlasting Father, the Prince of Peace' – Isaiah 9:6. That was Isaiah prophesying about our Lord

Jesus before He was unveiled to man. But with all that revelation, some professing Believers do not accept Jesus as the Almighty God. Humanly, it's impossible to understand and that's what makes God the Almighty. Understanding the Trinity is a miracle, that's why you need the Holy Spirit. I come from a strong Islamic home. My late father was a military officer. He had his military assignment, but was also the head of all Muslims in the Sierra Leone Army – he was an Alhaji, he went to Mecca; to the Kaaba stone. But on his dying bed, he was listening to a Christian radio station; Believer's Broadcasting Network – BBN 93.0 FM. One of my Christian sisters was also preaching Christ to him and I want to believe he accepted Jesus as Lord before his departure. Growing up, as a teenager, some of my elder sisters converted to Christianity and started walking me into Church services. But my mind was still Islamic-contaminated. I lived with my siblings and two of them who were committed members of the New Testament Bible Church continued indoctrinating me on the teachings of Jesus Christ. But there was something about their doctrine I could not understand. They emphasized Jesus as God, which I found difficult in accepting, considering my Islamic background – I questioned, 'How could Jesus be the son of God and at the same time Jesus being God'. Then, I held on to some of the Quranic teachings which says 'Gul gu ah la hu ah had, ar la wu samad, lamu ar laid ihn wa lamu u lad, wa lamu ar kula hun kufu wan ah had', meaning 'God has no child and no parent. He's all sufficient and there's none like Him'. I believed in the monotheism of the Almighty God and so that revelation of Jesus Christ further walked my human reasoning into a path of spiritual confusion. I argued with my sisters, using the Bible, as I repeatedly unveiled Scriptures that seemed to contradict their teachings. So my sisters could not get me to understand that, which acted as a stumbling block to my desired salvation. To verify the true nature of Jesus Christ, I then started reading the Bible personally. That was the first time I read the Holy Bible from the Book of Genesis to Revelation. And as I read, I asked the Almighty God to help me understand the true identity of Jesus Christ. During that period, I abstained from all worldly pleasures, including fornication which was my major weakness. I even got separated from my then-girlfriend, as she could not cope with that lifestyle. At some point, she thought I had started dating someone else. But I remained focused and permitted nothing to impede my spiritual exploration. I would be in my bedroom, locked up, researching about Jesus Christ from the holy Scriptures. As I read, I got attracted to Isaiah 9:6, a Scripture I would always remember which I would state again, 'For unto us a child is born, unto us a son is given. And the government shall be upon his shoulder, and His name shall be called Wonderful, Counsellor, the mighty God, the everlasting Father, the Prince of Peace'. That was Isaiah prophesying about the true identity of Jesus Christ, before His physical revelation on earth. But even with that Scripture, I remained in a state of incomprehensibility, as I struggled to remove the satanic veil from my spiritual optic lobes. I got further confused, as, in one instance, Jesus would be referred to as the Son of God, and in another, He would be designated God. As I continued, I discovered another Scripture that says, 'I am in the Father and the Father is in me. He that hath seen me hath seen the Father' – John 14:9-10. But with all those Scriptures, my thirst for the divine truth remained unquenchable and as I continued, I asked the Almighty God to help my unbelief, as I wanted to know the true way of worship and have a healthy tie with my Maker.

One afternoon, as I read, lying on my bed, I saw myself walking on a strange solitary path. It was so lonely and clear, that my eyes could laterally notice an emerging object out of a normal human purview. Suddenly, a being appeared onto me from a location I couldn't even trace. The seemingly radiation from the personality I saw was ineffable. He appeared like a human, but His features could not be figured out, as the intensity of the illumination that emitted from Him could not be measured on a human scale. The ambience transmuted and all I could sense was the enticing presence of a holy personality. I could not resist the emission from that supernatural being and bowed down on my knees, without my control, in divine submission. Just at the point of kneeling, I felt the right hand of that supernatural being on my head and simultaneously realized myself in bed, with the Holy Bible on my chest. Tears rained down, from my eyes, as if I had lost a very precious relation or friend. Instantaneously, I discerned that supernatural being as the son of man who was slain on the Cross of Calvary. I recognised Him as the

Son of God through whom we find eternal life. I identified the lion of the Tribe of Judah who defends us from satanic intrusion. He revealed Himself as the Alpha and Omega who is the beginning and end of all creation. And immediately, I accepted Jesus Christ as the Almighty God, and Lord and Saviour of my Life. If you asked me how I knew He was Jesus, I couldn't explain. If somebody asked me why I believed He is God, I couldn't explain. Why? It was a miracle. But one thing I know, whenever Jesus appears to you, He would let you know He's Jesus and you would understand His true identity, without unbelief. Jesus transformed my heart. He renewed my mind and regenerated my spirit. The Islamic veil was immediately expunged from my spiritual visualization. The next morning, I explained my first encounter with our Lord Jesus to my elder sisters, as we all were living at our father's residence in Freetown. They laughed and replied, 'Thank God, you would now believe'. Some days after my encounter with our Lord Jesus, one of my nephews invited me to their annual church event tagged 'Encounter'. It was about a week-meeting, with conferences in the morning and revival services in the evenings. Truly, I had no intention of attending those meetings, as I was focused on consolidating my relationship with Jesus – reading the Bible and praying fervently in my bedroom. But on the last day of the 'Encounter' revival services, I was troubled in my spirit. It was about 5:00 pm and the revival services started about that time. I was reluctant to go. I thought the event had already commenced and by the time I would be there, it would already have been past 6:00 pm and I would have had no sitting place. 'Encounter' was widely attended by residents of Sierra Leone. But some foreign occupants attended as well. That year, it was hosted at the Miatta Conference Centre in Freetown. And when gone after 5:00 pm, it was difficult to get a seat in the auditorium. But my spirit refused to remain at rest until my mind concluded to be at that evangelical meeting. I arrived at Miatta Conference Centre at about 6:00 pm and the hall was already clustered with congregation. The only location where I found a seat was out of the hall, downstairs, where I could only view the man of God via a projector screen. I saw only one seat when I arrived as if it was reserved for my occupancy. At a point, the man of God made an altar call, inviting members of the congregation who wanted to receive the baptism of the Holy Spirit. During my biblical research, I learnt about the Holy Spirit, but could not understand and never remembered having a taste of His baptism. I wanted to yield to the altar call to get a practical feel of the holy spiritual baptism, but I was a staircase down and thought by the time I would get there, the prayer could have ended. My decision kept swinging on a pendulum, as my passion for the holy baptism continually overwhelmed every element of consideration. And as I pondered, a supernatural force lifted me off my seat and I saw myself climbing up the stairway, walking towards the altar, without my control. It was like being remotely controlled by an intangible electronic system. I made an advance to the altar, from where the man of God was discharging his spiritual assignment. He started praying and as soon as his hand made contact with the head of the person next to me, my legs couldn't support my physical stature and I dropped on the floor. But I immediately fought and regained my original standing position. When the servant of God stretched his right hand over my head, a beam of light with very high intensity appeared in my view, as my eyes remained in closure. I then screeched in an unknown tongue. It was like an earthly language unknown to me. The whole auditorium was quiet and even the sound of a coin could be likened to that of a rocket propelling grenade. Nobody, not even myself understood my utterance and as soon as I was about to realise myself physically, I heard a loud voice say 'Speak'. I then began to speak in the English tongue, which was an interpretation of what I revealed in the unknown tongue. The message was about the end-time. Jesus says, 'My children, I love you. Love me. Don't you love me? Worship me. Don't you want to worship me? This is the end-time...'. After that spiritual revelation, I came back to my physical senses and realised I lay on the floor. The ushers pulled me up, but as soon as they released me, I ramped down to the floor, as my physical strength to support my phenotype was overwhelmed by the spiritual encounter. The ushers then supported me to my seat. After the service, I walked home, as my house was not too distant from the Miatta Conference Centre. And as I walked, the revealed end-time message constantly re-echoed in my ears. Normally, when I went out and returned home to my bedroom, I knelt in front of my bed in prayer. So as I got into my bedroom that night, I knelt and held on to the bed frame. The bed vibrated, with my whole body shaking, and convulsion is the best term I could use to help you envision my then physical state. I couldn't pray. I just laid in bed, under the anointing, until the next morning. Since then, the gift of tongues and interpretation, dreams and visions, began to manifest in my life. Before my encounter with Jesus, my mind was already made up to become a Christian. But I only understood and accepted Jesus as God when I had a visual encounter with Him. Does it mean you shouldn't accept Jesus as God, until you get a visual encounter with Him? No! In different situations, Jesus operates differently with different personalities. He works with us in different forms to erase our unbelief. To some He would appear. To others, He would send His servants. He might send an angel. He could just touch your heart. And in other instances, He might use a Christian friend. But my encounter teaches you that you need the spirit of the Almighty God to help you understand His true identity. This, you can verify in 1 Corinthians 12:3 which states, '…no man can say that Jesus is the Lord, but by the Holy Ghost'. Generally, in the Kingdom of God, you need to believe before you see, as God wants us to walk in faith. But if you're swimming in a pool of doubt, ask the Almighty God with an open heart, He would help your unbelief. Jesus always appears on assignment. And whenever you get a visual encounter with Him, He deposits something into you – a gift. Isaiah prophesied about the true identity of our Lord Jesus Christ and it manifested. The existence of Jesus on earth reveals the true nature of the Almighty God, as verified in Colossians 2:9 which states, 'For in him dwelleth all the fulness of the Godhead bodily'. Jesus carries the total presence and nature of the Trinity. The Father, the Son and the Holy Spirit are fully revealed in Jesus. He only took up an earthly suit to relate with humanity, as only Jesus could represent that perfect sacrifice to reconcile man and the Almighty God. In His encounter with John, Jesus says,'I am Alpha and Omega, the Beginning and the End, which is, which was, and which is to come', revealing His identity as the Almighty God – Revelation 1:8. Great servants of God prophesied about the true identity of our Lord Jesus, but that was Jesus himself revealing His true personality.

Thomas appealed to not only see the print of the nails in Jesus' hands but to put his finger in them and thrust his hand into His side because he had doubts about the resurrection of our Lord Jesus. He only believed after that verification – John 20:24-29. But the Almighty God operates in many other ways different from Thomas' situation. A local church hosted an event and I was invited to the revival services, together with a few of my siblings. It was about five days of revival services. On the third day, about two hours before the commencement of the meeting, we were at home and one of my sisters asked, 'Samou, Muslims believe Jesus has the power to perform miracles, but they don't believe He died and resurrected, how about that?' My sister had converted to Christianity as well, but like me, her mind was influenced by the Islamic principles. She believed in Jesus as the Son of God, but had some reservations on some Christian concepts, which infected her belief. And for that, doubts continually showed up in her mind which finally prompted that question. I replied, 'No matter what anybody believes about Jesus; if he doesn't believe Jesus died and was resurrected, his belief about Jesus is in vain. His unbelief about the death and resurrection of Jesus Christ nullifies every other belief he has about Jesus. It's the resurrection power of Jesus that empowers Christianity – you must believe in the death and resurrection of Jesus'. My sister couldn't ask further questions about the resurrection of our Messiah, but from her face, I could sense traits of doubt running through her mind. We got ready and left for the revival service. In the service, the choir led us into a worship session and there was a physical manifestation of the presence of God, during which I uttered an unknown tongue. After that session, the servant of God asked the congregation to close their eyes and join him in prayer. As soon as my sister closed her eyes, she saw Jesus in a sparkling white robe, walking around us. Instantaneously, she understood, and believed in the resurrection power of our Lord Jesus. Since that encounter, the gift of revelation overwhelmed her. John encountered Jesus, as explained in the Book of Revelation. But today, many Christians do not believe in heavenly revelation, probably because they're not the channel. If you have a healthy relationship with our Lord Jesus, you should be able to recognise the difference between a satanic revelation and a revelation from the Almighty God. If you can't, then pray and ask the Almighty God to help your unbelief. But no matter how anointed you are, if you only accept what's personally revealed to you, then you're walking in a state of unbelief no different from Thomas. The Almighty God abhors working with a man who walks in unbelief. God offers different gifts to different Christians, so that when we work together, we form a perfect team to achieve our goal, which is to bring sinners to repentance and accept our Lord Jesus as the Messiah of the world. But if you reject holy spiritual revelations because your human intellect doesn't comprehend, then, unknowingly, you're truly living in unbelief. The Holy Spirit teaches us through the Bible, He teaches us through personal encounters, He teaches us through messages from others, He teaches us as He desires. The relation between Christians and Christ is 'belief'. It's 'belief' that establishes a link between Jesus and His followers. So, divine separation begins when 'Believers' begin to interpret the Word of God with different meanings.

Satan is deceitful! The first promise the heavenly Father made to humanity when He offered Jesus as sacrifice is tied to our belief. In the sixteenth verse of John, Chapter three, the Scripture says, 'For God so loved the world that He gave His only begotten Son, that whosoever believeth in Him, should not perish, but have everlasting Life'. This is the Almighty God's eternal promise to man, driven by man's belief. And if you recall the incident in the garden of Eden, you would realise that the first tool Satan uses to fight against humanity is unbelief. This explains the relationship between condemnation and redemption. To be redeemed, you have to believe. And unbelief implies condemnation. But in this end-time, our Lord Jesus wants to restore His stolen children. He wants to fix the unbelieving infirmity. He wants to bring His people together – in His kingdom. The world would only be truly saved when Christians are united. But how can we be unified when we work in different beliefs? There is only one Jesus. There is only one Holy Spirit. There is only one heavenly Father. So where do you get the opposing beliefs from? We must extricate the spirit of unbelief from the Church and see our Lord Jesus as He truly Is. Satan keeps fighting to stop you from entering into the eternal promise of the Almighty God but by the power of the Holy Spirit and in the mighty name of our Lord Jesus, if you're walking in unbelief, the spirit of unbelief would leave you now and you would be redeemed by the blood of the lamb that was slain on the Cross of Calvary.

Opposing the truth is a satanic trait. Satan's dialect is full of nothing, but lies. Be vigilant! Remain sober and remember; unbelief is a satanic deposit. Reject it and enjoy a healthy relationship with your Maker.

Chapter II

The Will

When you submit your will to the will of the Almighty God, His will becomes your will.

Satan battles to override man with the spirit of unbelief, but when he fails, he applies other strategies to capture the will of man. The devil cannot control you until he gains access to your will. But he does it surreptitiously. Satan employs sin to distract, deceive and dehumanize humanity. Sneakily, he fights to walk you into an impure path that offers him your right to make functional decisions. Every man has a weakness. You have an elastic limit. And whenever you're stretched to that limit, surviving only becomes real if the Almighty God replaces that weakness with His strength. If He doesn't help your weakness, you run into your plastic region – your breaking point. So, what Satan does is, he attacks to push you into your plastic region. And if your bond with the Holy Spirit is not strong enough, it becomes impossible to understand that strategy and consequently, your spiritual strength transforms into human weakness. Satan overpowers you and slowly you become spiritually depleted.

Three Wills operate on earth – the Will of God, the Will of Man and the Will of Satan. All occupants of heaven, including the angels, operate in the Will of God. Lucifer functioned in the Will of God, but when he rebelled, he was cast out of heaven, together with his demons, and his Will became his own – Revelation 12: 7-10. Lucifer, then ceased to operate in The Will of God, as rebellion is not an element in the heavenly jurisdiction. And that choice of Lucifer to fight against the Almighty God is the will of Satan. Now, Satan's objective is to oppose human activities wrapped up in the Will of God. The will of Satan is to destroy God's human creation. When the Almighty God formed Adam and Eve, they were operating in His will. Man had a healthy tie with his Maker. As the first human-existing couple, Adam and Eve were submissive to their Creator. Every activity they fulfilled was in keeping with the desire of the Almighty God. But what happened? Why the change? When Satan succeeded in diving them into a river of disobedience, the holy covering dropped off their eyes and they could recognise the existence of good and evil – Genesis 3:22. Adam and Eve were evicted as well, from the garden and since then, man ceased to operate in the Will of God and became independent in his decision. Like Satan, man obtained his own will when man rebelled against the Almighty God. All forms of disobeying the Almighty God are considered rebellious, as man was designed to stay in a path that doesn't contravene the Will of the Most High. So, whenever you violate the instructions of the Almighty God, He sees you as teaming up with Satan, walking out of His will and into the will of Satan.

In Genesis 1:3, God says 'Let there be light', and there was light. The Almighty God commanded the existence of light in the heavens and on earth to illuminate the habitat of humanity. In the Book of Genesis, we see how God demonstrated His will in His creation. He displayed His power to make. He commanded things to happen, as His spirit moved and they happened according to His will. When Jesus existed on earth as man, Satan fought to artfully capture His will. After fasting for forty days and forty nights, Satan offered Jesus three different packages of physical temptation enclosed in spiritual deception – Matthew 4:1-11. Satan pronounces, 'If thou art the Son of God, command that these stones become bread'. Also Satan tempted Jesus to cast Himself down, if He is the Son of God, as it is written, God would send His angels to catch Jesus so that He wouldn't dash His feet against the rocks or fall to the ground. Further, Satan promises Jesus the world if Jesus shall bow down and worship him – God forbids. In the first two instances, Satan declares,' If thou be the Son of God', and in the third, he says, '...if thou shall bow down and worship me'. Satan knew Jesus is the Son of God. He wasn't trying to prove it. He knew! He was only cunningly fighting to acquire obedience from our Lord Jesus – God forbids. This, Satan demonstrated in the third attempt. He clearly stated, '...if thou shall bow down and worship me'. That was Satan's objective – to get Jesus to bow to him. Satan unfolded the camouflage in the third because the first two hidden strategies failed. Remember, sin is not only disobedience to God, but obedience to Satan as well. Satan hustled to seize the will of our Lord Jesus by two hidden strives encased in human hankerings – ego and love for affluence. In this contemporary age, some Christians could have undermined their spiritual capacity and challenged Satan by saying, 'Yes, I am a child of God. I would jump and the God I serve would send His angels to save me'. Others might have replied, 'You're no match for me, Satan. I will jump and nothing would happen to me', forgetting that the Almighty God should not be employed as a specimen, especially in a satanic research. Sometimes, people misconstrue the concept of faith. There are situations in which God says, 'Prove me', like in the principle of tithing – Malachi 3:10. But the Almighty God is just. When man received his own will, He wrapped it up in human senses. Even as a Christian, there are situations in which you employ your human senses and there are others in which you invoke the spiritual. Generally, you employ the spiritual where the physical could not survive. The Almighty God wants you to walk in faith. You cannot work with God without faith. You worship Him even though you can't see Him. You talk to Him when you're not even sure He hears you. You make a request to Him and whether He grants it or not could only be verified by a physical manifestation. With all those suspensions, you talk to Him. Why? Because you believe He exists and you have faith in Him. You believe He's your Creator. You believe He hears you when you talk to Him. You believe He responds when you make a request. But the concept of faith should not be abused. You cannot say God would deliver you and so you jump into a lake of fire, even though you knew the consequences. How could you run in front of a vehicle running at $250 kmh^{-1}$ and say, 'My God would save me'? Generally, the Almighty God supports you in situations beyond human resolution. He steps in when your human efforts fail. That's why your will envelops your intellect, it envelops your intelligence, it envelops your power to make choices. And so you need to employ your will to make choices that support the campaign of our Lord Jesus. There is no trouble the Almighty God cannot deliver you from. But you do not need to investigate whether or not He is God when you truly know Him. He might see it, not only as a test but also as a form of impudence. He might see you as not trusting in Him. If you know who God is and are doing something irresponsible to prove He is God, it seems as mockery. So remain cautious of how you apply the principles of faith. You can demonstrate the power of the Almighty God to Unbelievers, to help walk them into the kingdom of heaven. But a Christian trying to personally exhibit the existence of God by obeying Satan may end up in a demonic domain. Some others may have opted for worldly gains and traded their will. Satan does everything in his capacity to capture your will. The devil might have offered you the world, as he promised Jesus. But until you renounce it, the end would be eternal torment. Jesus demonstrated He's heavenly focused. When humanity understands that sin should not only be viewed as disobedience to God but obedience to Satan as well, then their Christian journey becomes a better path to eternity. Satan was cunningly fighting to access the will of Jesus by getting Jesus to obey his satanic supplications – God Forbids! But Jesus, with an overflow of the Holy Spirit, discerned Satan's strategies and rebuked him. The devil fled, as he realized Jesus is grounded in spiritual principles and understands His assignment. Sometimes, the will of our heavenly Father seems tough. If we go to the Book of Matthew, Chapter 26:39, we see that even Jesus cried onto His Father to re-examine the sacrificial part of His assignment. He says, '…Oh My Father, if it be possible, let this cup pass from me'. But Jesus continued, 'Nevertheless, not as I will, but as thou wilt'. Jesus, existing in human flesh, subjected His will to the Father. He acknowledges that the Father's Will is supreme. Satan cannot control you without your will. And he only captures your will, when you allow his strategies to entrap you. Christians are supposed to operate in the will of the heavenly Father. Yes, it gets threatening sometimes, but you must remember the Covenant of Salvation that glues us to the Almighty God and remember our assignment – the Great Commission. You must prove to that dragon that you understand the principles of heaven and remind him of the sacrifice Jesus made on the Cross of Calvary. In The Lord's prayer, Christians recite,'…thy will be done, on earth, as it is in heaven …'.That's a common and a very strategic prayer in Christianity.

But do you truly apply it? The will of the heavenly Father is to do what He says. His will is for man to stay away from satanic practices. His will is to destroy the works of Satan. His will is to do what the Bible teaches. His will is to worship Him. As Satan needs your will to deceive you, the Almighty God also needs your will to save you. In Acts 13:22, God says, 'I have found David, the son of Jesse, a man after my own heart, which shall fulfil all my will'. David's will was to do the will of the Almighty God. You must submit your will to the Almighty God and allow Him to use you as He chooses. Do not allow Satan to subdue your will. Apostle Paul realized the benefits of living for Jesus. His will was to preach the gospel of our Lord Jesus. He fought to get innumerable souls born into the kingdom of heaven. He was truly focused on Jesus. After his encounter with our Lord Jesus, Paul's will intertwined with the will of our Lord Jesus. That's why he declares, 'For me, to live is Christ, and to die is gain' – Philippians 1:21. Paul preached without fear. He knew the God he served. He did not fear to die for the gospel. Because he was confident he would be in a better place after his planetary existence. Like Paul, every Christian shouldn't fear death. You should preach the Word of God without fear. You should preach Christ with boldness. Do not employ your will to carry out the will of Satan, as Satan's will is to set humanity against the Holy Divinity.

'Wills' are truly knotted to the spiritual. The will of man is resident in the veiled man, guarded by the human soul. That's why people largely depend on your actions to interpret you. They see your deeds as a demonstration of your will. Mankind sees your actions as your desires, which can be misleading though. Like Wills, there're three major Spirits that exist on earth – The Spirit of God, the Spirit of man and the Spirit of Satan. In Matthew 17:14-18, a lunatic, possessed with the spirit of Satan, existed. Operating in the will of Satan, he sometimes fell into the fire and sometimes self-immersed in water. He couldn't operate in his will. But when Jesus appeared, Jesus cast the demon out of him. The lunatic was restored and started behaving normally. How? The Spirit of God ejected the spirit of Satan out of his human spirit and his will was retrieved. In Matthew 9:32-33, a dumb man, possessed with the spirit of Satan was conveyed to Jesus. Again, Jesus commanded the devilish spirit out of that man and he began to speak. The man had the desire to speak, but couldn't because his will was captured by Satan. Many people operate in similar situations. Unknowingly, their will has been subjugated by Satan and they behave in contravention to their normally desired actions. Sometimes, people do things and believe it's their desire, not knowing their will has been replaced by the will of Satan. And so Satan remotely controls them without their knowledge. The will of Satan does nothing of eternal benefit. So, whenever you carry out activities that oppose the principles of Christianity, you need to make a check and uncover the hidden strategies of Satan. The will of God never inspires you to oppose the principles of heaven. When Satan captures your will, he becomes the master of your desires. His desires become your desires. When you act, you may believe it's your desire, not knowing you're fulfilling the disparaging commands of Satan. Man and Satan were created by the Almighty God. So, we see that the spirit of man and the spirit of Satan are inferior to the spirit of God. Hence, the will of God is superior to the will of man and the will of Satan. However, the Almighty God allows the will of Satan and the will of man to exist because His word is His word and He wants to prove the loyalty. The will of Satan cannot be changed – it's set. Satan knows no repentance. He is on earth to kill. He is here to steal. He is here to destroy. But man has a choice to modify his will. You, now know, the difference between good and evil. You have a choice to make a change now. You have a chance to submit your will to the will of God. But after life on earth, only The will of God exists. The Almighty God is going to subdue the will of man and the will of Satan. On earth, you are free to do whatever pleases you. But in eternity, you're confined to the dictates of the Holy Supremacy. Satan employs different strategies to capture man's will, as he wants to control your life on earth before the end of time – his time is short – Revelation 12:12. That's why our Lord Jesus is fighting so hard to save humanity before the end of existence on earth. And that must remain the objective of every Christian. Christians must fight hard to win as many souls as they can. Every soul is important to our Lord Jesus and if you're following Jesus, His desire must be your desire. His will must remain your will. Satan employs so many hidden strategies to capture man's will. He applies so many concealed methods to walk man into sin.

In the neutral state, Satan is wiser than man. That's why he succeeded in deceiving the first created couple – Adam and Eve. In human strength, Satan is more powerful than man. That's why he controlled the demon-possessed guys. The Almighty God created man in His image, but He created man a little lower than the angels. And remember, Satan was a holy angel. But Jesus came to envelop us in the will of God, as we would only be wiser than Satan when our will is wrapped up in the desires of the everlasting God. Man has the power to make independent choices. He can choose between good and evil – man has a will. But man's will can be influenced by either the Almighty God or Satan. When man's spirit is possessed by Satan, man operates in the will of Satan. And when the spirit of God is resident in man, man operates in keeping with the will of God, as He advises him uprightly and helps him to recognise the strategies of Satan. Sometimes, people carry out actions they know are satanic and desire to make a halt. Some would make every effort to refrain, but the more they try, the more the margin between their desire and the satanic action increases. And consequently, they tag it an addiction. They couldn't stop because, unknowingly, the spirit of Satan is resident in their human spirit and so he manipulates them. You would only be able to operate in the Will of God when the Holy Spirit is resident in your human spirit. The will of the Almighty God is for you to enjoy an eternal life. He wants you to succeed on this planet and live with Him in heaven, forever and ever. Satan chooses to rebel against the Almighty God. And so, his will on planet earth is to kill, to steal and to destroy man, as he wants to take humanity with him to eternity. The Almighty God loves man so much and Satan knows it. That's why the Psalmist says, 'What is man, that thou art mindful of him?' – Psalms 8:4, Hebrews 2:6. The Almighty God loves man so much. Why? I couldn't justify. All I know is, He loves us, even before He created us.

Devoid of the Holy Spirit, the will of man on earth is to satisfy the flesh. The first act of Adam and Eve when they ate from the tree, in the garden of Eden, was to find themselves clothing. They realized they were naked because they walked out of the will of the Most High. They realized they had the power to make independent choices. But that independence invited demonic dependence. And until man is set free by our Lord

Jesus, man remains in the satanic sphere. That's what happens when you turn your back on Jesus. You realize you've got the power to make independent choices, but all in the name of satisfying the unsatisfied mortality. Walking in your own will comes with consequences. You become prone to Satan's strategic attacks. And with your human strength, Satan capturing your will is like a new born baby learning to cry. You would face obstacles you cannot overcome. When the prodigal son left his father's house, he thought he was grown. He thought he could handle his affairs of life. But he later realized that even ordinary servants of his father could father his material longings. Why? Because they lived in his father's will. He had to return with a transformed heart. He walked back home in repentance, to continue walking in the will of his father. Sometimes, when your human senses begin to mature, you begin to think you can do it yourself until you begin to encounter realistic complications. The prodigal son had everything he needed when he walked in his father's domain. But he decided to walk into his own will and later realized the covering over him had been detached. He acknowledged that his perceived material guard was nothing more than a cosmetic infrastructure. Many times, that's how many behaved to the Almighty God. They turn their backs on Him. They ignore their Creator and think they can do it all, only for them to realize that the foundation to a building would remain a supporting assembly.

Now, you can see the relation between man's will and the will of Satan. Both man and Satan achieved their will as a result of disobedience. But the difference is, Satan's will is unchangeable. He would never repent. His destiny is set. He has a specified period, after which his true identity will be revealed to those who consider him a spiritual giant. He is doomed. But man can transform man's will. You have a chance now and our Lord Jesus is ready to embrace your will. Jesus is waiting for you to walk into His will. Do not subject your will to Satan. Allow the will of the Almighty God to be done on earth, as it is in heaven and enjoy sweet eternity with your Creator.

We would now take a deeper look at the Will of Independence.

The Independent Will

The Almighty God doesn't need man to exist. He is a Sovereign God with an independent will. He does what He wants without external limitation. God can only be limited by Himself. He created man not because He needed man, as He can exist alone. He created man because He loves man. And so man was a major element in the creation plan of the Almighty God. When Lucifer was formed, the Almighty was delighted to keep him in His will. It wasn't His thought to see Lucifer walk out of His holy presence. However, when Lucifer operated in the will of God, he had options. But even in the Almighty God's domain, there are actions you take that hurl you into appalling reactions. And it was one of those choices made by Lucifer that led to his eternal eviction from heaven. When God made man, His desire was for man to continue walking in His will. But like Lucifer, man also had options. Man functioned in the will of God but had choices within God's will. And as I revealed, even in God's territory, there are choices you make that sail you into devastating consequences. Remember, God instructed man to eat from every other tree, but not from the tree of knowledge, of good and evil. God can institute a locking mechanism, prohibiting man's access to the tree. In other words, even if man made an advance to feed from the tree, he could've been supernaturally impeded. In that case, there would have been no need to relay a precautionary command. Our God is all powerful. He could have precluded man from yielding to the will of Satan, as well. But He knew He provided man alternatives and that man could eat from the tree if he wanted to, that's why he cautioned him. But the difference between the options or choices God offered man initially is that man operated within the will of God and his options were limited. Now, man is walking in his own will; an independent will, with unlimited options. Man now has the power to whatever choice he desires. That's why man can even choose to submit his will to Satan. In that case, the will of man would be limited to the will of Satan. And man's will can only be limited again to the will of God if man submits his will to Him. God gave man options because He loves man. His desire was for man to operate in liberty, but he got disappointed in the garden of Eden. Man and Satan tendered applications to receive their independent wills, by disobedience. However, the will of man can also influence the will of God. God's will is to work with man, but that would only solidify when man cultivates an ideal platform, except on special assignments. So God responds to man according to the will of man.

Now, what does it mean to be spiritually independent?

The Cost of Spiritual Independence

Having an independent will drives man with a high cost. It feels good when you can make your own choices. You feel great that you have unlimited options. But you must realize there are consequences to every choice you make – whether beneficial or detrimental. When you are growing up in your father's home, you get to a point at which you feel you can make independent decisions. You feel you know what's good for you and what's not good for you. Assuming your father says,' whenever you want to go out, I'll give you my car and a driver, but please don't drive'. You say, 'Okay, Papa'. The first time you don't drive. The second time you go out with the driver, you do not drive. And the third time, you get influenced by a friend. You drive and run into another vehicle. You suffer an injury that can only be fixed with the support of your biological father. The prodigal son left his father's house. He thought he was grown enough to live independently. He thought he was matured enough to make good choices. He left. At some point, he realised that even his father's servants can lead a better life than he could. He realised he couldn't do without his father. He had to return in repentance. Before you decide to live in independence, think logically. Think carefully. By nature, man is weak. Now, man has an independent will, but man cannot survive independently. Satan has an independent will, but his independence is destructive. The will of man and the will of Satan are offsprings of God's will, as they were created by Him. So, no matter how independent man and Satan are, in the end, God will subdue them. When man operates independently, he becomes disposed to the control of Satan. Satan is wiser than the independent man and so he manipulates his will. Now, man can make independent choices, but man is in trouble. Man walked out of the will of God, but his will can be easily captured by Satan. And the end can be eternal damnation. That is the price for man's spiritual independence. Man was created a holy immortal, but lost it to Satan. That's why instructions, especially the Holy divine, must be followed. And until man returns to his Maker, man would always be influenced and conquered by Satan. Satan's destiny is set. The consequence for his independent will is settled. He is condemned, already.

Disobeying the Almighty God is identical to obeying Satan. It is satanic!

Chapter III

The Power of Fornication

The spirit of God and the spirit of Satan are two opposing Spirits brawling to gain total control of the human spirit. As Satan makes demonic advances, the Holy Spirit reveals his strategies. Satan gets mad. He becomes frustrated and struggles to establish divine separation between man and the Holy Spirit, to preclude revelations of his devilish instrumentation. Satan understands the Scripture, as he was a principal personality of the hosts of heaven. He knows how to apply specific scriptural strategies to specific situations.

When our Lord Jesus was physically departing the earth, after completion of His sacrificial ministry, He promises to provide His followers another Comforter, which He fulfilled. He says the Comforter, which is the Holy Spirit, shall be with us and in us – John 14: 16 - 26. Jesus continued, 'Howbeit when He, the spirit of truth, is come, He will guide you into all truth: for He shall not speak of Himself; but whatsoever He shall hear, that shall He speak, and He will shew you things to come. He shall glorify me: for He shall receive of mine, and He shall shew it unto you '– John 16: 13 - 14. Satan comprehends that quote. He understands that promise made by our Lord Jesus, and He understands the operations of the Holy Spirit. Satan knows that the Holy Spirit will reside in man, and will reveal all his demonic strategies to humanity. But Satan, just by himself, has no power to deprive humanity of the indwelling of the Holy Spirit. So, he stimulates man to violate the heavenly command that supports operations of the Holy Spirit in man's life. Satan cannot nullify the power of the Holy Spirit. But he can invalidate the operations of the Holy Spirit in your life when he succeeds in driving you to break the healthy bond that glues you and the Holy

Spirit together. There are many ways Satan can influence man to offend the Holy Spirit. But in 1 Corinthians 6: 18-20, Paul says, 'Flee fornication'. Many, including Christians, argue that sin is sin. They emphasize that all sins are the same. They believe there is no distinction. Yes, when you sin, you have sinned. All forms of sin are satanic and bear identical eternal consequences, but sins are classified. And the different categories of sin influence your life on earth differently. Sins can be classified into Forgivable and Unforgivable.

Forgivable Sins

These are sins that can be forgiven when you accept Jesus as Lord of your life and submit to Him. Forgivable sins can be erased by repentance. When you confess them to the Almighty God and make a turnaround from them, He can forgive you of them. But these can only hold when you accept our Lord Jesus as Lord and Saviour of your life. Unwittingly, forgivable sins can walk you into eternal destruction. Many believe the Almighty God forgives when they repent and ask for mercy. They believe the grace of God is always there to wipe out their transgressions. Yes, by His grace, the Almighty God can forgive you when you drop off your suitcase of iniquity and ask for His mercy. But is grace a license to sin? Grace is undeserved favour from the Almighty God – it's not an authority to immorality. Many continue in forgivable sins because they know it's erasable. But you can sin to an extent that the Almighty God closes the gate of grace over you. The Almighty God offered Jezebel space to repent of her fornication and other satanic practices, but she remained defiant – Revelation 2:21. Jezebel wasn't out of this world. She was alive. She was still living on earth when the Almighty God made that declaration. Jezebel continued in fornication and adultery to an extent that the Almighty God vowed to destroy her. And God did destroy her.

There are three major categories of Forgivable Sins:

The Creative Sin

Prior to Adam and his wife, Eve, defying their Creator in the garden of Eden, the Almighty God prophesied they would die. Some viewed that declaration as physical death. But, in real sense, that vow speaks of the spiritual. It talks about divine separation of man from the Almighty God. When a creature becomes spiritually separated from his Creator, he dies. So, the creative sin was introduced from the initial existence of man when man followed Satan, into the path that drowned his magnificent destiny. That sin was created by man and passed onto every man created on earth – it's an inherited sin. The Book of John, Chapter three and verse sixteen, reveals that the Almighty God sent his only Son, Jesus, to the world because He loved the world and that whosoever believes in Jesus will not perish, but have eternal life. The Almighty God emphasized that when you believe in Jesus, His Son, your eternity will be celebrated in dignity. This explains that the creative sin walked man into an eternal death. And so the only way the creative sin can be erased is by believing in Jesus. It can only be forgiven when you accept Jesus as the Son of God and the Messiah of the world. The creative sin can only be deleted when you acknowledge Jesus as Lord of your life. There is no other means by which the creative sin can be forgiven – it can only be washed away by the blood of Jesus. Creative sin can be forgiven only once, and that's all. It's instantaneous. You don't ask God to forgive creative sin. As soon as you accept Jesus as Master of your life, it becomes deleted automatically and you're set free from the stigmatisation in the garden of Eden.

Fornication

Paul reveals the human body is the temple of the Holy Ghost, created to glorify the Almighty God. The human body, soul and spirit belong to the Almighty God, as Jesus paid the price on the Cross of Calvary. All other sins committed by man are not against the body, but fornication violates the human body, which is supposed to be the earthly residence of the Almighty God - 1 Corinthians 6: 18-20. The Holy Spirit does not live in church buildings – Acts 7:48-50. The Holy Spirit lives in us, Christians. When Jesus was departing the earth, after His resurrection, He promises to send us another Comforter, The Holy Spirit, which shall be with us and in us, to guide us into all truth. The Holy Spirit resides in you to teach and remind you of the principles of heaven. The chief role of the Holy Spirit is to guide you from sin, by revealing Satan's strategies and advise you on a Christian path. But when you yield to the demand of fornication, you defile the earthly residence of the Holy Spirit. The Holy Spirit gets exasperated and leaves, as He cannot occupy a defiled human temple. The Holy Spirit doesn't live in a filthy vessel. As I mentioned, when you don't have the Holy Spirit, Satan is wiser than you. And so his demons can then rush into you, as they desire. Your body now becomes a temple of Satan and he becomes your chief adviser. Satan begins to advise you into iniquity. He begins to teach you activities that oppose the principles of heaven. Your life becomes full of immorality, as the Holy Spirit is no longer in you to help protect your preordained destiny. Our God is Holy, so He resides in an unpolluted body. Fornication runs you into other sins and can destroy the rigidity of your Christianity. Fornication has natural devastating effects like bad health, infection, teenage/unwanted pregnancy, etc. But in this context, I am focused on its spiritual consequence on man – how it directly affects your relationship with the Almighty God.

Other Sins

Other sins are forgivable sins outside the Creative and Fornication category. They include lying, stealing, murder and other forms of abuse against humanity. Other sins like lying and camouflaged stealing might be considered insignificant, but they slowly remove your Christian apparel. For instance, it's so easy to tell a friend you didn't buy a drink when your inner man is overwhelmed by culpability. It's so easy to pick up meat from a cooking pot at home, without authorisation from the chef. It's relatively easier to use an item that doesn't belong to you, without permission from the possessor. Generally, some Christians view some other sins as trivial. But gradually, they eat up your Christian values and can easily walk you out of Christianity. Other sins can be nurtured to other forms of sin that might be contagiously shattering. For example, lying against someone can lead to his murder. And his murder can lead to further conflict, if avengers rise on his behalf. This can even escalate to a fight of ethnicity and national divide.

Unforgivable Sins

Unforgivable sins are unforgivable. These are sins that immediately assign you a satanic nomenclature. Unforgivable sins cannot be erased, as their designation is condemnation. Whether you proclaim Jesus as Lord of your life, it doesn't matter — they cannot be deleted. No amount of repentance or submission to our Lord Jesus can delete them. Many are ignorant of unforgivable sins. Some are packaged with the knowledge but do not believe there are sins the Almighty God do not forgive. Our God is merciful, but His word remains His word. The same God who says, 'Thou shall love thy neighbour as thyself', is the same God who says, 'Thou shall not commit adultery'. God can forgive and God cannot forgive. The same God who says to Abraham 'I will bless thy seed' is the same God who says to Jezebel 'I will destroy you'.

There are two major categories of unforgivable sins:

The Holy Ghost Offence

In Matthew 12:31-32, Jesus says, 'Wherefore I say unto you, all manner of sin and blasphemy shall be forgiven unto men: but the blasphemy against the Holy Ghost shall not be forgiven unto men. And whosoever speaketh a word against the Son of man, it shall be forgiven him: but whosoever speaketh against the Holy Ghost, it shall not be forgiven him, neither in this world, neither in the world to come'. Jesus made that pronouncement when the Pharisees accused Him of using satanic powers. They emphasized Jesus used the power of Beelzebub, the prince of devils, to cast out demons when he healed a man of blindness and dumbness. In other words, when they say He cast out demons by the prince of devils, they referred to the Holy Spirit as a satanic spirit – God forbid. Jesus demonstrated mysteries by the power of the Holy Spirit, which bewildered the mental strength of the Pharisees. Their human senses couldn't decode the secrecies of heaven, and that kept them crawling in the unbelieving trajectory. In the Trinity, only Jesus is our advocate. That's why the life of Jesus on earth is our perfect model. Jesus forgives man when man hurts Him, but the Holy Spirit doesn't forgive. The Holy Spirit guides us. He empowers us to defeat sin. The Holy Spirit resides in man and so would make a perfect witness against man, when man assaults His spiritual personality. Christians and Unbelievers must acknowledge there're unforgivable sins. Similarly, in the contemporary age, when a true servant of God operates, he works with the empowerment of the Holy Spirit. And so, if you accuse him of employing demonic powers, you're committing the same offence as that of the Pharisees. There are false prophets, but until revealed by the Holy Spirit, abstain from the accusation. Do not accuse a preacher of being a false prophet when you have no verification of his satanic operation. There's a difference between 'I don't believe' and 'it's a lie'. When you say 'I don't believe', it implies you have reservations about a concept, which can change with proof. But when you say 'It's a lie', your judgement is unleashed already. That's why as a Christian, you need the Spirit of Discernment – to distinguish between a man of God and a man of Satan.

The Mark of the Beast

In Revelation 13:16-18, we see, 'And he causeth all, both small and great, rich and poor, free and bond, to receive a mark in their right hand, or in their foreheads: And that no man might buy or sell, save he that had the mark, or the name of the beast, or the number of his name. Here is wisdom. Let him that hath understanding count the number of the beast: for it is the number of a man; and his number is six hundred threescore and six' – 666. In Revelation 14:9-13, the Almighty God revealed to John, 'if any man worship the beast and his image, and receive his mark in his forehead, or in his hand, the same shall drink of the wine of the wrath of God, which is poured out without mixture into the cup of His indignation; and he shall be tormented with fire and brimstone in the presence of the holy angels, and in the presence of the Lamb: And the smoke of their torment ascendeth up for ever and ever: and they have no rest day nor night, who worship the beast and his image, and whosoever receiveth the mark of his name'. The Mark of the beast – 666 would be the invisible currency during the great tribulation after Jesus has received His unblemished church. Satan will be authorised by the Almighty God to rule the earth, after the rapture, and you would not be equipped to engage in any form of trade without Satan's identity. But the 666-token medium goes with devastating eternal consequences. Accepting the mark of the beast is an unforgivable sin. Do not accept any form of technological inscription on your body, whether embedded chip or otherwise. Satan is very tricky. He knows humanity is already aware of the number of his name. He would devise a hidden algorithm to enable you to accept his number. When you receive the mark of the beast, no matter how you cry, no matter how you pray, heaven would remain closed over you because you've endorsed Satan as lord of your life. When you're engraved with the mark of the beast, you have made a declaration to heaven that Satan is your master and you have denounced the Almighty God as your Maker.

Sins can also be classified as:

Sin of the Mind

This is a very powerful strategy employed by Satan. Sins of the mind are intangible. They are abstract. They are mental. There are some thoughts, until you translate them into actions, they remain in you. They remain intent. They remain a plan. Nobody might know about them, but only you and the Almighty God. These include inner actions like jealousy, envy, hate and other inner violations. The human spirit can carry out tasks by itself, but remember that when your spirit is devoid of the Holy Spirit, Satan is wiser than you and influences the state of your mental capabilities. But even if your thoughts or actions are not influenced by Satan, as long as they violate the principles of Christianity, they are classified as satanic and regarded as disobedience to the Almighty. Satan speaks from outside to manipulate Christians full of the Holy Spirit, and if you're not sensitive, he remotely controls your mind and influences your decisions. This is one of Satan's major strategies against Christians washed in the precious blood of our Lord Jesus. Sin of the mind slowly translates into physical sins. When you become jealous or hate someone, you begin to find ways to oppose him in the physical. Sometimes, the sin of the mind begins by what you see. A man can be in his bedroom, alone, thinking about sleeping with a lady he saw the previous day. It can also come from what you hear. You can hear someone talking pornography and you begin to imagine filth. A pretty lady might touch you and you rush into arousal. The sin of the mind can be devastating! Ignore it!

Physical Sins

Sins committed in human actions are considered physical. You see them in the physical. People do them. They are tangible. Armed robbery is an example of physical sin. But many are into stealing and do not even realize it. Some realize but consider it insignificant. When you're an employee and take what doesn't belong to you. When you take what your company doesn't offer you. When your mum is cooking and in her absence, you pick up meat from the pot without her permission, all are classified as stealing. Murder is a physical sin. When you put an end to someone's existence on earth, it's considered a physical sin. Generally, for physical sins, you get physical consequences on earth, even though there can be eternal penalties as well. Some go to jail for stealing and the rest of their lives amount to a negligible value. Some acquire lifetime incarceration for murder, whilst others run into a death sentence, taking an earlier exit to eternity unprepared. Physical sins can be intentional or unintentional. Many murders are premeditated. But there are some that are fortuitous, even though they can emanate from deliberate actions. For instance, you can hit someone on the jaw as a form of penalty for misconduct, without the intent of exterminating him, but may end up bidding farewell into the world of the deceased. Hence, physical sin can have both physical and spiritual/eternal consequences.

Sin of the Mind vs Physical Sin

Generally, sin begins as a thought. It begins in the mind and later crystallises. Sin of the mind translates into physical sin. But for some, until you apply them in the physical, they remain thoughts. When a man wants to steal, it begins in the mind. For a veteran, as long as his plan is designed, he may not consider before going into action. But for a baby thief, he may begin to wobble between application and abstinence. If his desire for application overrides the drive for abstinence, the implementation of his design translates into the physical and is classified as sin. But for fornication, the sin begins in the mind. Sometimes it translates into a physical sin, other times it remains in the mind. But even if it doesn't solidify, as long as the sexual imagination resides in your mind, it's considered a sin of the mind. So fornication can be a sin of the mind, and it can also be a physical sin. You can be in your bedroom alone, thinking of sleeping with a lady you saw the previous day. Sometimes, you even strip her naked in your mind. Refrain from a mental engagement that can neutralise your purity. A very committed Christian lady notified me that she gets negative thoughts she didn't like. She says filthy/sinful thoughts just show up and asked me how to deal with that. I said to her, 'The first thing is to recognise them as satanic and rebuke them instantaneously. You do not dwell on them. When your optical senses capture satanic scenes, get your eyes off and hurriedly unseat them in your mind. Pray and immerse yourself in the word of God. Read your Bible or other Christian articles, if feasible. You can turn on Christian gospel songs. Just engage in something ecclesiastical and keep yourself busy, as sometimes many satanic thoughts rush into an unproductive mind. So, whenever satanic thoughts come up, rebuke them and immediately envelop yourself in the Word of God'.

The Unknown Sin

This, I characterise separately, but includes all categories of sin. It can be a forgiving sin. It could be an unforgiving sin. It could be a sin of the mind. It can be a physical sin. Unknown sin refers to when you walk into sin unaware. You know it's sin, but you didn't know when you committed it. In other cases, you do it, but don't know it's sin. Picking meat from your mother's pot without permission can be an unknown sin. Borrowing someone's pen and not returning it can be an unknown sin as well. Talking ill of someone is a sin. Watch yourself and stay away from unknown sins.

Dealing with Unknown Sin

Recognising unknown sins can be difficult. So firstly, you need to pray for the Holy Spirit to help you identify them. And whenever you pray, ask God to shower you with His mercy regarding unknown sins. If you do it deliberately, it's not unknown. The Almighty God reads your heart. He reads your mind. He interprets your thoughts, even before you think. Hebrews 10:26 talks about 'Wilful sin'. Wilful sin is a deliberate sin. It's a sin committed by a Christian – someone who's born again, washed in the blood of Jesus and knows the truth of the gospel of our Lord Jesus. It says if you continue in sin, after having the knowledge of the truth of our Lord Jesus, there is no more sacrifice for you. In other words, the blood of Jesus would not speak or work for you anymore. So as a Christian, you need to remain careful in your Christian journey.

We've scrutinised the different categories of sin. We've identified the disparities and recognised their point of intersection. The power of fornication has been unveiled. And it's evident that fornication drives the Holy Spirit away and walks man into a satanic trajectory. The Holy Spirit is supposed to be your guide in Christianity. But when He departs from you, who would perform the role of His guide? Fornication, like its specialised counterpart adultery, is a special category of sin. Fornication is a class of its own. Fornication has negative natural effects like bad health. You can get infected sexually and capture a terminal disease. Fornication can lead to unwanted pregnancy and other forms of immoral consequences. But in this context, I am focused on its spiritual effect on humanity. Fornication defiles God's temple and the Holy Spirit doesn't dwell in a contaminated vessel — He leaves. Our Lord Jesus reveals the Holy Spirit should be our counsellor and shall guide us into all truth. He will show us things to come. But if He leaves, who would be your counsellor? Who would guide your path? Who would reveal Satan's strategies to you?

David cried to God to create in him a clean heart and renew a right spirit within him. He appealed to the Almighty God to not cast him away from His presence and not take His Holy Spirit from him. David cried to God to restore onto him the joy of His salvation and to uphold him with His free spirit – Psalms 51:10-12. David recognised the relevance of the Holy Spirit in his Christian journey. When David talks about renewing a right spirit within him, he's talking about his human spirit. The human spirit has its characteristics. For instance, someone can have a feature of anger. So to renew your spirit can imply replacing that anger with a form of docility. If your anger is satanic, our Lord Jesus can easily flush it out. But in genetic cases, the Holy Spirit contains it differently. When your anger wants to show up, the Holy Spirit could say 'calm down'. He could advise you to be pacified. Your anger might be natural, but Satan can employ it to manipulate you. Anger can lead to murder. It can lead to making decisions that would walk you into everlasting regret. It can even lead to your earthly expiration, as you can be stabbed in a fight, for instance. So, you can see that the Holy Spirit advises and protects you from all sins, including fornication, when you have Him. The Holy Spirit is the best adviser you can ever get, as He is always there. He is the best counsellor you can even accommodate as long as you have a healthy relationship with Him. Or else, the Holy Spirit will get replaced by a satanic spirit and all your counselling would remain clouded in demonic mislead. When the Holy Spirit is absent in your life, sin becomes your living pattern.

The Holy Spirit and the spirit of Satan cannot live in the human body at the same time. When satanic spirits are cast out of a man, they become vagabonds. They become homeless. They wander around and when they can't find a place to reside, they return to the man and if they find it empty, if they don't find it occupied by the Holy Spirit, they bring along seven more spirits and the man becomes more infected satanically – Matthew 12:43-45. The human spirit, by itself, is depleted – it can either be possessed by a satanic spirit or the Holy Spirit, as a function of your will. That's why when you don't subject your will to the will of the Almighty God, Satan can easily possess you. The Holy Spirit doing work in your life doesn't mean He is resident in you. The Holy Spirit is omnipresent – He is everywhere at every time, but shows up in specific cases, as instructed by our Lord Jesus. He only resides in you when you invite Him, and upon the command of our Lord Jesus. When a satanic spirit is cast out of a man, his human spirit becomes purified – it becomes clean of impurities but prone to further demonic contamination. If you invite the Holy Spirit, He is ready to reside in you and work with you. But if the satanic spirit returns and doesn't find the Holy Spirit in you, he, together with more demons, rush into you and comfortably make their abode. You become a demonic habitat and Satan becomes your chief adviser. There are human counsellors, people who can advise or calm you down, but what if they're not available at the time of the incident? What if they don't know about the incident before its occurrence?

When I just got saved, some years back, it was difficult for me to submit. Fornication was my major weakness. But the Holy Spirit supports us when we're ready for change and submit our weaknesses to Him. The Holy Spirit is my friend. I know how He operates, as I've had both good and bad times with Him. One of the major ways He talks to me is through dreams and sometimes through visions. Other times, He speaks to me as I walk, work, eat and drive. And many times as I write. But whenever I get into fornication, I dream and I don't remember. I see visions with no heavenly interpretation. My writing skill deteriorates as I don't hear from the Holy Spirit. I continue fornicating with no regret which is a devastating state a backslidden Believer can get into. I talk to God and I don't get a response. I become spiritually deaf and walk into divine blindness. We worship during church services, and I don't even desire to connect to the Trinity. That's the worst height a fractured Christian can ever attain. But some years ago, I was getting ready for a three day fasting. And the Holy Spirit says, 'No, Forty days'. I said, 'What Lord?' He says, 'Forty days of fasting and prayer', and revealed that it's necessary to help me deal with the spirit of fornication. I'm an electrical-engineer and was working in the mine then. I was worried about how to handle that on-site. But when God schedules a task, He empowers you to accomplish it. Then, I asked the Holy Spirit to strengthen me as I began. I started the fasting process on-site and the only thing that made me know I was fasting was my eating plan and I lost considerable weight. But in terms of hunger, I was fine. Sometimes I even forgot I needed food. And God was constantly communicating with me as I worshipped Him daily. On completion of the forty-day fasting and prayer, my illegal passion for the opposing sex ceased. When I finally turned away from fornication, the situation becomes the opposite – I lost taste of sex. And now, my will is to maintain a healthy relationship with the Holy Spirit at all times. Because when you have Him, He guides you into perfection. Life without the Holy Spirit is an undefined risk. The Holy Spirit knows the end from the beginning. So He reveals occurrences to you, even before they happen. Satan understands the power of fornication – and he knows the Almighty God always stands by His word. Fornication breaks your spiritual bond with the Trinity. When you have no relationship with the Holy Spirit, Satan is wiser than you and manipulates you as he desires. He gets you into unacknowledged demonic metamorphoses. Sometimes, even when the Holy Spirit is gone, Satan continues to offer you make-up revelations from his demonic mental strength. He manipulates you into believing that your gift still operates by the power of the Almighty God, even when the Holy Spirit is no more in you and with you. But that truth can only be revealed when you have a healthy tie with the Holy Spirit. It's the Holy Spirit that relates man to the Trinity, through faith in our Lord Jesus. Fornication makes you insensitive to the voice of the Almighty God. You become spiritually deaf to the words of our Lord Jesus and Satan begins to take the place of God in your life. The devil becomes your god. He begins to speak deceptively to you. When you want to make meaningful decisions, he helps you make decisions that would seem temporarily good, but ends in eternal catastrophe. He keeps you in situations that might seem excellent in terms of worldly standards but produces everlasting destruction. Satan is wicked!!! Jesus knew that without the Holy Spirit, Satan would conquer man. That's how he defeated Adam and Eve. The human spirit, by itself, is weak – weaker than the spirit of Satan. We only become powerful than Satan when we have an indwelling of the Holy Spirit. Man only becomes brilliant than that old serpent when the Holy Spirit lives in man. Remember, Satan was in heaven. He was so loved by the Almighty God to an extent that he thought he could dethrone the heavenly Father – God Forbid!!! The Father empowered Satan, whilst in heaven. And even after his rebellion, God did not retrieve the power from him. He only kicked him out of His residential domain. So Satan is still in operation of that temporary infected power. That's why, in Revelation 12:12, heaven says, 'Woe to the inhabitants of the earth and of the sea! For the devil is come down unto you, having great wrath, because he knoweth that he hath but a short time'. The Almighty God knew man was defenceless, considering the power He gave to Satan. And that's why He sent the Holy Spirit, to help us repel the attacks of Satan, and destroy his works. Satan's power is subject to the Almighty God's power because his power emanated from the everlasting God. When you run into fornication, it's either you don't listen to the Holy Spirit or you do not have a healthy relationship with Him. Satan has no control over a purified vessel. If you're a Christian, do not blame the devil for mishaps because the Holy Spirit reveals all of Satan's strategies to you, which makes you wiser than him. But you have the choice to reject or accept – you have a will. Christians are supposed to control Satan and his demons. We're supposed to speak to Satan and his demons and they should obey. But that control would only be activated when you allow the Holy Spirit to reside in you. If you repel your indwelling of the Holy Spirit, instead of you controlling Satan, Satan would control you. During fornication, your body is defiled – your spirit becomes open. Satan infiltrates at any time. Demons can rush into you as they desire. And when they do, you now become a temple of Satan, instead of the temple of God. You become non-receptive to the voice of God and Satan uses you as he chooses. You become insensitive to the voice of the Holy Spirit and all other sins become your lifestyle – lying, stealing, extensive fornication, with no regret. So, you see that fornication invites all other forms of sin.

Nevertheless, you hear of some anointed servants of God falling into fornication and adultery. Why do you think a man of God, with an overflow of the Holy Ghost, a man who opens blind eyes, a man who even raises the dead, falls into fornication or adultery? Why do you think a servant of the Most High who teaches the word of God violates the same word he teaches? Why do you think an anointed man of God, washed in the blood of our Lord Jesus, falls into sexual sin? The anointing does not delete your sexual appetite – it can quench it, but pops up intermittently, as you would need it for your spouse. Sometimes, when a man of God becomes spiritually matured, when he gets deeper into his assignment, he becomes confident and satisfied with his spiritual status. He becomes complacent. He believes he's at the point of perfection and thinks the probability of Satan tempting and overpowering him is zero. But you need to realize that no matter how anointed you are, Satan would come and you must always be ready and submit your human spirit to the spirit of the Almighty God. After fasting for forty days and forty nights, Satan still tempted Jesus. The anointing supports you. The Holy Spirit guides and advises you. But you have the responsibility to obey the Holy Spirit and reject Satan. Many male Christians, including servants of God, have female Christian friends. Yes, you can have a female friend but your interaction must remain on a platform with pillars that remain fortified, even on the day of the strongest wind. When the both of you continue to be in a solitary environment, especially a bedroom or any other confined space, the probability of you running into sexual sin increases with time. Your erection does not require your permission, and its major passion is self-satisfaction. Sometimes, your erection originates from your thoughts, satanic thoughts, but you don't necessarily have to say 'yes' to get an erection. With all the anointing, when you get an erection, your male organ desires to imbibe a delicious meal. The brain begins to process the request and your blood flow becomes commensurate in readiness to receiving the opposite organ. You can't stop the request because it's a reflex action. Your biblical knowledge, including scriptural references, that opposes fornication begins to disappear from your mental archive. When you're in a confined space, a solitary one, with the opposite sex, especially one you're not biologically related to and one you would have a soft spot for, sexual continence can only be exhibited when your human spirit yields to the counselling of the Holy Spirit. You can endure for a day or two, but continuity can walk you into a path that requires repaired repentance. Avoid continually spending time with the opposite sex, you're not related to biologically or through marriage, in a closed region. Your spiritual legs can be broken. This goes for both sexes – male and female.

Satan comes, but the Almighty God would not allow you to be tempted beyond that which you are able – He would always make an escape route – 1 Corinthians 10:13. But you have to follow His instructions. The Holy Spirit does not support any form of sin. Allow Him to live in you. Listen to Him and enjoy a healthy relationship with the Trinity.

Chapter IV

Demonic Control

'Get thee behind me, Satan!' Those were the words of our Lord Jesus when Satan attempted to cunningly capture His will, by offering Him the world, after fasting for forty days and forty nights. Satan tempted Jesus in three different situations. He asked Jesus to convert stones into bread. He tested Jesus to cast Himself down from a high pinnacle. He asked Jesus to fall and worship him. In all three advances, Satan revealed supporting references, interweaved with promises, to Jesus. He requested Jesus to prove He is the Son of God. He says angels would not allow Jesus to fall to the ground. Satan offered Jesus the world if Jesus falls and worships him. The scriptures Satan quoted were valid. Satan had the power to offer Jesus worldly treasures. But, what was Satan trying to achieve? Why did he unveil valid scriptures and promised Jesus huge treasures?

The Holy Spirit helps us repel Satan's attack, but doesn't inhibit Satan from coming. Jesus has an overflow of the Holy Spirit. Everything Jesus does moves with the Holy Spirit. But Satan repeatedly made advances in a fight to control the will of our Lord Jesus. So, no matter how anointed you are, Satan would attack. But Jesus repeatedly proved to Satan that He understands spiritual principles more than Satan. He continually reminded Satan that His spiritual capacity and level of wisdom would always drown Satan in a sea of irrelevance. The physical existence of Jesus on earth demonstrated true Christianity. Jesus is our perfect model. Satan would come. But we, Christians, must repeatedly remind Satan that we are true followers of our Lord Jesus. We must continuously prove to Satan that with the support of the Holy Spirit, we understand spiritual principles more than him and in all his wisdom he's nothing more than a trivial element. When Satan ended his threefold temptation against Jesus, he departed for a season – Luke 4:13. That implies when Satan fails to capture your will in a moment, he leaves to develop other strategies and make a comeback.

Satan attacks in many ways. When he was kicked out of heaven, he was extricated with his team – the fallen angels who fought alongside him, in heaven – Revelation 12:9. These demons are continuously deployed in different locations to fulfil his satanic disruptions. Satan is tricky! Jesus assigned the Holy Spirit to reside in Christians to fortify their human spirits, so that whenever Satan makes his advances, he would face a heavenly challenge and man would continuously get the perfect guide. Satan knew that the best position to occupy is in man. That's Satan's best deployment. Sometimes, the Holy Spirit speaks to man from the outside, but that's occasional – on assignment. Satan operates synonymously, as well. But when you have an indwelling of another spirit, it translates into a lifestyle. For as long as a demon is resident in you, you align to his dictates because your will has been captured by Satan. But when he speaks from the outside, you have a choice. Satan was speaking to Jesus from the outside, employing scriptural references, but Jesus proved to Satan and humanity that He is the Word of God, without Whom nothing was made that was made – John 1:1-14. Satan made so many attempts to seize the will of our Lord Jesus. In Matthew 26:39, Jesus prayed, 'Oh my Father, if it be possible, let this cup pass from me'. Yes, those were the utterances of our Lord Jesus. But don't you believe Jesus knew the purpose of His physical existence on earth? Don't you believe Jesus understood His assignment before coming? Don't you believe Jesus knew His assignment was heavy before taking it up? He knew! But what happened? Why was Jesus complaining? Jesus was in depression because Satan was speaking to His spirit from the outside. Satan was struggling to destroy His assignment, by capturing His will. That old serpent was striving to splinter the resilience of our Lord Jesus. He wanted Jesus to give up, as he knew what would emerge from the successful completion of that assignment. Satanic spirit cannot infiltrate the personality of our Lord Jesus – God Forbid. But Satan kept making intermittent attacks against Jesus. When you're full of the Holy

Spirit, satanic spirit cannot enter you, so the devil speaks from the outside in an attempt to manipulate your will. When Jesus revealed the plan of His crucifixion and resurrection to His disciples, Peter rebuked Him, saying, 'Be it far from Thee, Lord: this shall not be unto Thee'. But again, Jesus replied, 'Get thee behind me, Satan' – Mark 8:31-33. It was Peter who uttered, but Jesus didn't say 'Get thee behind me, Peter'. He says 'Get thee behind me, Satan'. Why? Peter thought he loved Jesus so much and believed their physical separation would imply an eternal separation. He never knew the departure of Jesus was necessary to enhance their spiritual stature. He didn't want to lose Jesus, not knowing it was Satan speaking into his spirit, and he yielded. But Jesus recognised that strategy of Satan. Many times, Satan uses man to capture man's will. But Satan doesn't fight alone. He fights together with his dark angels – the demons. He deploys his dark angels into man. I refer to these men as demonic humans. And Satan employs these demonic humans to help carry out his demonic assignments.

In every setting, there must be an administrative infrastructure. There's need for a team to run the affairs of an organization. But selecting workers in the church is not supposed to be by the independent human intellect. The church is not a secular domain. Church authorities, whether administrative or otherwise, must be Christians and must remain Christian. You don't appoint someone as a worker, just because he is your friend. You don't ordain someone a ministerial authority because he gives the biggest tithe. The twelve Apostles said, 'Wherefore, brethren, look ye out among you seven men of honest report, full of the Holy Ghost and Wisdom, whom we may appoint over this business' – Acts 6:3. When the disciples wanted to ordain spiritual workers, they didn't just appoint. They hunted men of honest report, with wisdom and full of the Holy Spirit. So in addition to other ministerial criteria, workers must be full of the Holy Spirit – that's the first criterion. The Holy Spirit must remain the drive of every ministerial activity. You must allow Him to fully handle all Christian engagements, as embarking on a ministerial journey without the Holy Spirit leads to a satanic destination. Even great servants of God can be frustrated when they work with empty workers – Satan uses those empty workers as access points to hit at God's servants. So, to select any member as a worker, the Holy Spirit must approve. You submit a recommendation and the Holy Spirit remits a confirmation. Servants of God are full of the Holy Spirit. And must remain sensitive as the Holy Spirit offers them direction – He wouldn't allow them to jump into err, if they would stay glued to His counselling. But some do not seek the Holy Spirit's approval for ministerial appointments. And Satan, cunningly, unleashes his demonic humans into the church. That's one of the major reasons servants of God face so many troubles in the ministry. That's why some workers chase other workers to have illegal affairs in the church. That's why some workers arrive late to perform their roles. That's why some are late for meetings. That's why some workers misuse church funds. All these mishaps transpire because workers are empty. You cannot stop Satan from attacking, but you can stop him from manipulating you. You can repel him. And for as long as the Holy Spirit remains in charge of your undertakings, you wouldn't remain a victim of satanic interruptions.

Church leaders must pay special attention to the choir and intercessory teams, as they are at the extremes of the spiritual. The choir initiates the heavenly invitation. They replenish the altar to welcome our Lord Jesus and His hosts of heaven, during services. The intercessory team takes the lead in defending the church against satanic intrusions. They help uncover Satan's strategies, destroy his demonic altars and repel his devilish attacks – they constantly engage Satan in battle. So when the choir and intercessory team get infected, the church hangs on a fragile spiritual pillar. Jezebel, who called herself prophetess, was employed by Satan to extinguish the assignments of God's servants – Revelation 2:20. These were not false prophets. They were genuine servants of God. But Satan manipulated them because he succeeded in capturing their will. Jezebel repeatedly offered them food sacrificed onto idols and they munched with satanic satisfaction. She succeeded in getting them to yield to her fornication offers. Satan can also use empty workers to cultivate demonic disruptions in the church. He ordains 'preachers' to help win man, as well. The Bible warns us to not believe every spirit, but that we should test the spirits whether they are of the Almighty God, as many false prophets are unleashed into the world by Satan – 1 John 4:1. Christians must remain sober and vigilant. That's why you need a discerning spirit, and must depend on the Holy Spirit in everything you do.

Some time ago, I met with a young lady in the northern part of Sierra Leone, who used to visit a guy regularly. And one day, I had an opportunity to have a close chat with her. Suddenly, my burning desire to investigate her amplified. Previously, she briefly informed me that she's a Christian, and I jumpstarted from there. 'How is your Christian life?' I asked. 'Fine', she replied. I responded 'wow!' And I continued, 'How strong are you?' She replied, 'I am strong, even if I tell you, you wouldn't understand, you don't know'. I said, 'Yes, I don't know, that's why I asked you'. As she was about to initiate her revelation, I developed a certain boldness, which was truly inspired by the Holy Spirit, and I reacted, 'If you lie, I would know. So, just say the truth'. And she started, 'I am the youth intercessory leader in our church. I am also a member of the Ministry Intercessory team. I am also...'And I replied, 'Hold on! Do you have a boyfriend?' She paused for a moment and with a defeated voice responded 'No'. 'Why?' I asked. She revealed she had, but they broke up about a year ago. Why? She said that, that, that...But that was someone chasing a man, in the name of a relationship. She chased the guy in the name of an affair. She knew the man was married, but he was living away from his wife, on a job. And many times, they were locked up in the guy's bedroom. However, I counselled her and noticed she stayed away from the man. How do you expect the church's growth? How do you expect to defeat powers of darkness in some ministries? How do you expect victory in a ministry in which an intercessory leader is busy sleeping with a man she's not married to? How do you expect a demonstration of the power of God, when an intercessory leader is secretly having an affair outside marriage? Ministerial heads must remain careful of how they appoint workers. You might end up appointing workers who pray against the church, instead of praying against dark angels. You could appoint workers who pray against congregational increase, rather than praying for soul-multiplication. You may admit workers who pray for demonic demonstration, instead of praying for the manifestation of the Holy Spirit. You might employ workers who invite curses, rather than blessings into the ministry. You would work with members who open the door to satanic operations. Soul gathering is not identical to soul-winning. An increase in ministry membership does not imply church multiplication. Some ministers are called by our Lord Jesus but as they carry out their assignments, they get distracted by Satan, as they offer him their will. Now, we hear of ordinations. You receive invites from ministers to be ordained. But do people understand what ordination is all about? The God we serve is the God of Covenant. When you are ordained, you enter into a covenant with the Almighty God. You agree to faithfully discharge your assignment, in spirit, in truth, and hence in holiness. So, when you break that covenant, the Almighty God deals with you, in keeping with your vow, and His word. It's your vow that would speak against you. Ministry is an assignment. It's not just another organisation. If you're not ready to work for our Lord Jesus, please do not accept ministerial appointments. But if you do accept, your life must speak Christianity.

Ministry belongs to our Lord Jesus. When Saul was persecuting Christians, Jesus roared, 'Saul, Saul, why persecutest thou me?' – Acts 9:4-5. Jesus didn't say, 'Why are you persecuting the Church?'. He didn't say 'Why are you persecuting my people?' He said, 'Why are you persecuting me?' Why? Christians are the body of Christ. Our Lord Jesus is the head of the Church. So when you persecute Christians, you persecute the body of Christ and hence our Lord Jesus. That's why when you mess up in the ministry you help bring shame to Christianity and fight to pull down the name of Jesus. But no man can pull down the name of Jesus. You can only succeed in pulling yourself down and push people away from the gospel, which you would account for. You might not be a pastor, you might not be a preacher, but as long as you are part of the Christian workforce, you are a minister of the gospel of our Lord Jesus, as all Christians are supposed to be part of the Great Commission Assignment – Mark 16:15. Ministry is a calling, no matter how small you see it, as every soul is very precious to our Lord Jesus. So pastors, evangelists, prophets and other specialised servants of God, allow the

Holy Spirit to help you make ministerial appointments, and we would all enjoy a healthy growing Church.

Humanity easily gets deceived by a flamboyant activity. So Satan employs camouflaged events of his dark world to keep man in bondage. He uses those activities as a snare to capture your will and control you. One of the ways the devil does that is to continuously set up activities wrapped up in satanic trepidation. In some cases, he hosts activities man thinks are enjoyable. In other cases, he organizes activities that implant fear into man, violating principles of the Almighty God. Generally, scary events are initiated by Satan.

There's a 'misleading myth' that Halloween is a Christian celebration. They tag it the 'Eve of All Saints Day, and All Souls' Day'. Halloween, a contraction of 'Hallow' and 'Evening', was established by a set of people who tagged themselves Christians. To them, Halloween represented a hallowed evening or Holy Eve. This is the first deception, supporting the fact that the Halloween celebration is of Satan. What makes Halloween holy? If we truly scrutinize the celebrating activities, we would figure out a lot of biblical contradictions.

Halloween is full of horror. It's full of scary activities, to fill man of demonic fear. Fear is of the devil! The Almighty God has not given us the spirit of fear. But of power, love and a sound mind – 2 Timothy 1:7. Man should fear God. But in that context, fear talks about respect for God. It signifies total love for the Almighty. It talks about reverence for God – Godly fear. Halloween does not offer man a sound mind. It offers a thrilled and unrest mind, expectant of ghostly attacks. Halloween does not offer love. It's a satanic event. You might see it as fun but can demolish your Christian foundation. And remember, scripture warns of jesting – Ephesians 5:4. The trick-or-treat identity of Halloween is another violation of the Holy Scriptures. When some Halloween celebrants stepped into a stranger's, they demanded to be treated, by offering candies and other forms of sweeties. And if you don't treat them, they trick you by discharging mischief. Is that a demonstration of love? The Bible cautions of anger, aggression and stealing. Scripture warns of mischief – Psalms 7:16. The trick-or-treat activity introduces children to barbarism, as well.

Halloween was being, initially, celebrated by people who believed the presence of ghosts would help their priests in predicting their future. They sacrificed animals and crops to their deities. The Almighty God cautions us to not offer food, or any form of sacrifice, to idols - Acts 15:29, 1 Corinthians 8:4. And He further commands we should worship no other god, for He is a jealous God – Exodus 34:14. God does not compromise His monotheism – He is and will remain the only God Almighty. The founders of that demonic event dressed in masks, believing that ghosts of the dead would appear on Halloween, and would recognise them as one of them, for fear. They believed the dead would help them in foretelling. This is another terrible lie. The dead has no power. Satan is the father of all lies – John 8:44. When you depart this world, there are only two eternal destinations – heaven and hell. When you make it to heaven, you enjoy eternal peace. But if you end up in hell, you gain everlasting torture. Once you're dead, you remain in your eternal residence. Man only has a will on this planet, that's why there's no repentance after death. In eternity, it's only Jesus who has a choice – all activities are dispensed in the will of our Lord Jesus. You're only remote controlled. So when people say they see ghosts, they actually see demonic spirits. Demons, sometimes, employ features of the dead to deceive humanity. When someone passes away, they can take up his form in counterfeit.

This Halloween demonic celebration is now related to modernity, especially when the Americans recognised it and now are practising it. They host parties, play games, tell scary stories, etc. But when you become a part of any Halloween celebration, whether partying or not, you share the detrimental eternal consequence. Some offer food, lit candles on the graves of their deceased, all in the name of appeasing them. They sacrificed to goddesses. So, you see how Halloween promotes idolatry. The Almighty God wants His name to remain glorified in everything you do. Natural and supernatural occurrences are non-coincidental. When God drops man into this planet, He drops him on purpose. So, your birth date is not a matter of random happening. It's pre-meditated by the Almighty God. As names, every date of birth has a spiritual significance. There are many dates on the human calendar, so when you're born on a particular date, it runs with huge importance and responsibility. I was born on 31st October – the Halloween Day, demonically celebrated by a set of people who profess to be Christians. There's only one goal of the gospel – to bring sinners to repentance, reconciling them onto the heavenly Father and glorifying our Lord Jesus. How does Halloween positively influence Christianity? How does Halloween help in soul-winning? Halloween is about dress-coding in representations of the dead. It's about celebrating Satan. And now, people are dressing in attires of the careers/professions they desire in the future. Others dress in apparel of their superheroes. All these are strategies of Satan to get more people involved in the Halloween celebrations, and cunningly they get initiated into his dark world. I used to celebrate my birthday in worldly affairs. Unwittingly, I was glorifying Satan during my birthday celebrations. But now, the Lord Jesus would receive all glory as I run into successive biological years. Celebrate your birthday in love. Celebrate your birth in purity. Celebrate in holiness. Glorify Jesus on your birthday anniversary. And let heaven celebrate you in return. By that, you let the Almighty God acknowledge He created a child who appreciates His handy-work.

Satan employs different strategies to capture the will of man. He has several strategies to control man. When you celebrate Halloween, you unknowingly, invoke satanic spirits, who become masters of your lives. The ultimate goal of Satan is to eternally separate man from his Maker. But Satan rarely unleashes direct confrontation. He develops techniques to deceitfully walk you into his demonic domain. Satan tagged Halloween as a 'Christian activity' to initiate 'suckling Christians' and Unbelievers into his fatal kingdom. One of the symbols of Halloween is a Jack-o'-lantern – a scary masquerade, verifying the satanic identity of that demonic celebration. Why do people dress in masks and masquerades? Masks are counterfeit representations – Satan uses them to deceive humanity. Masquerades are demonic applications, designed to entrap man into the satanic world. Halloween is one of the strategies of Satan to bring and keep humanity, even Christians, into his satanic world. Stay away from Halloween celebrations and keep yourself out of satanic trepidation. Kick Halloween out of your celebrations schedule and glorify our Lord Jesus in everything you do.

Recognise Satan's strategies and never allow him to control you.

Chapter V

Contaminated Doctrine

When Satan succeeds to infiltrate the Church, he employs different strategies to entrap Christians. Generally, Satan fights against humanity. But specifically, he focuses on Christians. He fights against the congregation of our Lord Jesus. He fights against persons full of the Holy Ghost. And intensely, he fights against Christians who understand his satanic strategies. Satan is not troubled about Unbelievers. The devil doesn't bother much about lukewarm Christians. He only reinforces his control of them. As I mentioned earlier, Satan's greatest attack is against the Church. When Satan penetrates the Church, he fights to contaminate the gospel of our Lord Jesus. And when Unbelievers get 'converted' through impure doctrine their spiritual desire becomes tailored to the demands of Satan. When Christians continue to absorb infected messages, they gradually walk out of Christianity. Satan initiates a drive to practise contaminated teachings and when Christians are ensnared, he cunningly sets them against the Almighty God. Ignorance is unacceptable to our Lord Jesus. Not understanding the gospel of our Lord Jesus would not save you from the judgement of Christ. Jesus makes it clear that the Holy Spirit resides in His followers to guide them into all truth. Listen to anointed preachers of our Lord Jesus, but you must depend on the Holy Spirit for understanding the truth. The Holy Bible is the constitution of heaven. The Almighty God judges man according to His word. So, whether you understand or not, His word remains His word. Naturally, when you violate a national constitution, you are prosecuted and investigated according to the laws of the land. The court doesn't care about whether you knew it was an offence or not. The judiciary tries to prove you guilty or not guilty.

Writing, including drawings, talking, singing and lifestyle are different forms of ministry carried out by Christians to spread the gospel of our Lord Jesus. Sometimes it's done live, other times through audio and video recordings. But the Holy Spirit has revealed that one of the most powerful forms of ministry Satan uses to fight against humanity is the singing ministry. Satan uses the Music Ministry to keep Unbelievers in his dark domain. Every talent the Almighty God offers man is to contribute to developing His kingdom. The everlasting God offers you the aptitude to help spread His word. He offers you talent to help win souls. But unfortunately, many utilize their talents to glorify Satan, and in many cases influenced by Satan himself. As the Almighty God ordains music ministers, Satan simultaneously ordains his own – they transmit songs that duplicate the gospel of our Lord Jesus, but with no holy spiritual relation. They do songs full of devilish manipulation. Music plays a vital role in the ministry.

When the Levites, together with their sons and brethren, lifted their voices with trumpets and other forms of instruments in praising and thanking God, the house of worship was filled with cloud. The glory of the Almighty God filled the sanctuary that the priests could not stand to minister – 2 Chronicles 5:11-14. The music ministry is very influential. In our time, there are reports of cripples running out of wheeled-chairs as music ministers sing. When sanctified ministers sing, when music ministers washed in the blood of our Lord Jesus raise their voices to exalt the name of Jesus, when you hear music ministers full of the Holy Ghost sing, accessing the throne of heaven becomes easier. But if your singing drive is a financial search, if your singing objective is fame and not to glorify our Lord Jesus, then you're a victim of Satan's musical strategy and would have to answer to our Lord Jesus.

Music is a powerful form of evangelism. But Satan employs hidden strategies to fight against music ministers ordained by our Lord Jesus. He fights to contaminate their messages. He influences them to release distorted songs. But Satan only succeeds in manipulating you when you offer him your will. Some gospel music ministers tend to copy secular music artistes. But music ministers must realize their assignment is sacred. They are not performers, they are not entertainers – they transmit gospel messages to bring Unbelievers into the kingdom of heaven and help keep Christians understand and continue glorifying the Almighty God. Music ministers are melodious evangelists. When you write songs, allow the Holy Spirit to guide you. Like any other form of ministry, one contaminated song can jeopardize the eternal destination of many Christians. That's why as a Christian, you must remain careful of the songs you listen to. Music contributes immensely to developing your spiritual stature. But when you absorb satanic songs, your spirit man nurtures a satanic physique. And every time you recite the words of contaminated songs, you are making a satanic confession that defines your spiritual passion. Be careful of the wording of the songs you listen to. Remain careful of the songs you sing. For instance, consider a song that says, '...come and change my destiny....' The destiny of every man is pre-designed by the Almighty God. Destiny is an assignment. Destiny is a calling. By satanic manipulation, your destiny can be deformed. Your destiny might be mutilated. So, you can ask God to fix it. You can ask Him to repair it. You can ask God to make your destiny happen. But asking Him to change your destiny implies you do not appreciate your assignment, even though you might not know it. But every Christian is supposed to know his assignment. You might be designed to become the most anointed preacher in your time, but there could be satanic hurdles you need to overcome. So don't ask God to change your destiny. Ask Him to make it happen, and as a Christian, you must learn to fight against satanic opposition. But some think their current states are their destinies. Satan strategizes to destroy every plan and establishment of the Almighty God. The devil continuously fights to thwart your destiny. Your destiny is your assignment. Your destiny is the purpose for which the Almighty God created you. We were created to carry out the Great Commission. Our assignments are tied to heaven. The Almighty God designed our destinies to contribute to soul-winning. You need to mature. Sometimes, some Christians misconstrue persecution as a distorted destiny. A Christian shouldn't cry about persecution. Do you remember what Jesus said to his followers? He said that His followers shall be hated of all men for His name's sake. But they that endure to the end shall be saved. As a Christian, learn to fight battles. You must fight to defeat the powers of darkness. You don't always need to complain to God. Another major function of the Holy Spirit is to empower Christians for the ministry. Jesus says we shall receive power after the Holy Ghost has come upon us – Acts 1:8. When you have the Holy Spirit, you have power. All you need is faith and command things to happen in the name of Jesus. So when you listen to songs, don't just be driven by the tunes, don't just be conveyed by the instruments. Don't just be moved by the sound. Carefully listen to the words, as Satan employs the music ministry to manipulate Christians. If you hear a song you like, carefully listen to the words. If they are Christian, that's good. But if infected and you would want to use them, you can modify the words as you sing.

Satan, tirelessly implements his strategies in a fight to tear the Church apart. Satan is crafty! When he deals with Unbelievers, he knows how to handle them. He knows the strategies to apply to keep them caged. And when he deals with Christians, he applies different strategies, to which Believers that are 'careless' easily fall. Satan knows Christians are full of the word of God. He knows the followers of Jesus are full of Scriptures, so he employs hardly decoded methodologies to capture the will of Christians. Satan introduces impurities into the Christian doctrine, which can only be revealed by the Holy Spirit. One of the major ways Satan contaminates Christian teachings is by causing Christians to interpret the word of God with different meanings. This leads to denominational disparities. But even some in identical denominations decipher Scriptures differently. And remember that one infected pill in your doctrine can invalidate your belief. One of the deceptions Satan uses against Christians is related to the word 'Works'. Many Christians believe we're not under the law anymore. They believe we're living in a dispensation of grace. Yes, we're living in a period saturated with the grace of our Lord Jesus. But we need to understand the essence and application of the grace we're talking about.

When the Pharisees heard about Jesus putting the Sadducees to silence, they assembled. Then one of them, a lawyer, tempted Jesus by asking Him which is the greatest commandment in the law. In response, Jesus, being immeasurably intelligent, revealed the first and greatest commandment which is to love the Lord with all thy heart, with all thy soul and with all thy mind. Jesus continued that the second greatest of the commandments is to love your neighbour as yourself. He emphasized all the laws and the prophets hang on to those two commandments – Matthew 22:34-40. Those were the revelations of our Lord Jesus. Every organized system is governed by laws and from that quote, we see that the Ten Commandments are a set of laws. We see that all instructions from heaven are wrapped up in these two Commandments – To love the Almighty God and to love your fellow man, including yourself. But what does it mean to love God? In John 14:15, Jesus says, 'If ye love me, keep my commandments'. Many Christians proclaim they love God. Many personalities declare they love Jesus. But Jesus says if you love Him, you'll keep His commandments – John 14: 15-23. You only prove you love Jesus when you obey His commandments. You cannot proclaim you love God and continually violate His instructions. If you say you know Jesus and do not keep His commandments, you call yourself a liar – 1 John 2:1-6. The love of God is fully revealed in you when you keep His words. You only get to a point of perfection when you trace the earthly curve of our Lord Jesus. Sin is not the nature of the Almighty God. Sin is the identity of Satan. You cannot profess you love God and ignore His commands. In Matthew 5:38-39, Jesus says, 'Ye have heard that it hath been said, An eye for an eye, and a tooth for a tooth. But I say unto you, that ye resist not evil: but whosoever shall smite thee on thy right cheek, turn to him the other also'. In the Old Testament days, when you amputate a man, you would be amputated as well. Whatever way you offend your fellow man, it would be reciprocated to you. These are some of the laws some set of Christians employ to justify iniquity. We're no more under the 'an eye for an eye' law. We're no longer operating in the 'tooth-for-tooth' law. But the doctrine of our Lord Jesus does not nullify the laws of heaven. It does not nullify the 'thou shall not steal' law. It does not invalidate the 'thou shall not commit adultery' law. It does not support murder. Jesus was preaching love. He was preaching forgiveness. Sometimes, in my closet, I worship the Almighty God, as I prostrate on the floor. This is one of the secrets to my healthy relationship with our Lord Jesus. I like worshipping the Almighty God in my bedroom, with worship songs, as I lay on the floor. Many times, I go for like an hour and be led by the Holy

Spirit. On a particular date, as I worshipped our Lord Jesus, my utterance translated from English into an unknown tongue – it sounded like the Chinese linguistic. And as I continued, the interpretation unfolded in the English mode of communication. The Lord says, 'My son, I have commissioned you to speak the truth, speak the truth, speak the truth'. The Lord continued saying, 'Any doctrine that supports sin is from the devil, any doctrine that supports sin is from the devil, any doctrine that supports sin is from the devil'. After those words, I realised myself in the normal physical senses.

The trouble many Christians are having is with the understanding of the word 'Holiness'. Holiness is defined differently by different Christians. This is the trouble in the Church – interpretation of Scriptures and this is causing immense problem amongst Christians. If all Christians depend on the Holy Spirit for interpretation, then we all would have one heart and one mind. Our Lord Jesus physically lived on planet Earth and He is our perfect model. His physical existence on earth demonstrated the true life of a Christian. Holiness is submission to our Lord Jesus. Holiness is not just about struggling to abstain from evil deeds. Holiness is about adhering to the counselling of the Holy Spirit – it's about spiritual purity. The Holy Spirit teaches you to not sin. He guides you in a Christian pathway, and as you apply His instructions, you become perfect, even as your heavenly Father is perfect. When you surrender to our Lord Jesus, He releases His Holy Spirit to reside in you. And the Holy Spirit teaches you the principles of heaven. So 'works', in that context, is when you do it without Jesus. 'Works' is when you continue fighting to obey the instructions of the Almighty God, without the help of the Holy Spirit. Some confuse the baptism of the Holy Spirit and Holiness. They believe just the baptism of the Holy Spirit makes them holy. Listen carefully, anything sanctified and certified by our Lord Jesus is holy. At the point of your Holy Spiritual baptism, you become holy. Anything satanic is ejected. But to continue in that holiness, you need to submit to our Lord Jesus. Also, some confuse the indwelling of the Holy Spirit and Holiness. You can have the Holy Spirit and not holy. The Holy Spirit comes to counsel us. He lives in you to guide you. He resides in you to walk you into holiness. He counsels you into perfection. But if you do not adhere to His admonition, slowly you get Him aggravated. He can choose to leave and unknowingly, you walk out of Christianity. So to remain holy, you need the indwelling of the Holy Spirit and stick to His counselling – this is the total submission to our Lord Jesus. Our God is holy. And He says, 'Be ye holy, for I am holy' – 1 Peter 1:16. To have a good and everlasting relationship with our Lord Jesus, you need the Holy Spirit. Jesus says, 'If ye love me, keep my commandments. And I will pray the Father, and He shall send you another Comforter, that He may abide with you for ever; even the Spirit of truth; whom the world cannot receive, because it seeth Him not, neither knoweth Him: but ye know Him; for He dwelleth with you, and shall be in you' – John 14:15-17. Holiness is just submission to our Lord Jesus – total submission. You would never be holy without the Holy Spirit. You would never be holy until you submit to our Lord Jesus. Did Jesus command any man to sin? No! All the commandments of Jesus warns man to abstain from sin. So, grace is not a license to sin. Grace offers you access to the throne of God. Grace allows you to be forgiven when you confess your sins and ask for mercy. Grace sets you free of the creative sin – grace permits Jesus to embrace you when you repent. Grace offers you redemption when you make a turnaround from satanic activities and accept Jesus as your Lord and Saviour. Grace doesn't command you to sin. Grace allows the Holy Spirit, which teaches you all things, to reside in you. Grace is not an authority to iniquity. The dispensation of grace is not a justification to sin. The works doctrine is a strategy of Satan to infect the Christian doctrine and walk immorality into Christianity. Even Paul reveals we're not under law – he says we're under grace. But he continued, 'What then? Shall we sin because we're not under the law, but under grace? God forbid.' – Romans 6:12-16. Apostle Paul explains sin should not reign in our mortal bodies and our lusts should not be satisfied. He warns that our bodies should not be used as instruments of unrighteousness, but as instruments of Righteousness – to glorify our Messiah.

Our Lord Jesus made it crystal clear that your light should shine before men, for them to see your good works and glorify your heavenly Father. Jesus did not come to destroy the law. Jesus came to fulfil the law. He says all His laws will be fulfilled before the end of the world. So, if you break His laws and teach men, your penalty awaits you and will be tagged least in the kingdom of heaven. But if you obey and teach men the laws of our Lord Jesus, you will receive your eternal reward and be considered great in the kingdom of heaven – Matthew 5:16-19.

The gospel of our Lord Jesus is the gospel of truth. It's the gospel of perfection – Matthew 5:48. One erroneous declaration can push millions away from the gospel of our Lord Jesus. Do not preach compromised teachings. Preach the gospel of truth. Your objective, as a minister, is to prepare humanity for eternity. Your goal is to help man spend eternity with the source of his immortality. So if you teach man to sin, the Almighty God would hold you accountable. Remember, any doctrine that supports sin is from Satan. Sin separates you from your heavenly Father. So, as you do ministry, write truth, talk truth, sing truth and live truth.

Chapter VI

The 'Judge Not' Slogan

'Judge not, that ye be not judged. For with what judgement ye judge, ye shall be judged: and with what measure ye mete, it shall be measured to you again.' – Matthew 7:1-2. This is a very popular scripture in the Christian domain Satan uses to add to the number of backslidden Believers and keep Unbelievers bound in iniquity. From that quote, an excerpt has been developed which is now a universal slogan. 'Judge Not' is a popular slogan Satan employs to promote heavenly disobedience. Satan knows our God is holy! The devil knows Christians must remain holy to maintain healthy relationships with their Maker. So in a fight to undermine that holy attachment, Satan manipulates biblical quotes to confuse baby Christians.

If we prudently make a deep study of the New Testament, we would realize that the gospel of our Lord Jesus is the gospel of judgement, enveloped in love. In the Book of Matthew, Chapter 11 and Verse 28, Jesus says, 'Come unto me, all ye that labour and are heavy laden, and I will give you rest'. In John 8:12, Jesus says, 'I am the light of the world: he that followeth me shall not walk in darkness, but shall have the light of life'. In John 6:35, Jesus says, 'I am the bread of life: he that cometh to me shall never hunger'. In all these scriptures, Jesus demonstrated love through beneficial conditional heavenly promises. He says, 'Come unto Me...'. He says, 'He that followeth me...'. He says, 'He that cometh to me...'. He says, 'He that believeth on me...'. But in Matthew 10:14-15, Jesus says, 'And whosoever shall not receive you, nor hear your words, when ye depart out of that house or city, shake off the dust of your feet. Verily I say unto you, It shall be more tolerable for the land of Sodom and Gomorrah in the day of judgement, than for that city'. And in

Matthew 13:41-43, the scripture says 'The Son of man shall send forth His angels, and they shall gather out of His kingdom all things that offend, and them which do iniquity; And shall cast them into a furnace of fire: there shall be wailing and gnashing of teeth'. We see that these latter scriptures are judgemental. The Almighty God loves man so much that He fights to retrieve His deceived creation. The desire of our heavenly Father is to live with His children, forever and ever, in His holy residence. He never intended to be eternally separated from His human creation. But man yielded to Satan, which established a supernatural barrier between man and his Maker. However, Jesus has paid the price for our redemption. Reconciling with our Maker is free. Free in the sense that we, humans, do not have to pay anymore. But in another sense, it's not free because someone settled the incalculable bill. Jesus paid an immeasurable price for us. It's like your biological father honouring a financial debt for you. You wouldn't have to pay a cent, but your father paid the price. So, to Christians it's free. But to Jesus, the cost is immensely high. Jesus was rejected. He was molested. He was humiliated because of you. But as Jesus did, you have to make your own sacrifices, as well. You cannot do what Jesus did. No man could do it. But you must do what you must do to restore that broken holy relationship. The beneficial promises of our Lord Jesus are conditional. When you fulfil the conditions of the heavenly obedience, you enjoy them. But when you violate, you face the satanic consequences. We all know how God destroyed Sodom and Gomorrah when they decided to glorify Satan through their immorality. They turned their backs on the Almighty God. They refused to recognise Him as their Maker and continued in satanic practices. They refused to repent and submit to their Creator. When you accept Jesus, you enjoy His love, but when you reject Him, you suffer His wrath. This is a judgemental teaching. Jesus was talking about what happens to disobedient children at the end of the world, or at the end of their earthly existence. When you accept His teachings, He draws you closer. But when you reject Him, He judges you according to your life on earth, in keeping with His word.

There are three forms of judgement man needs to understand:

Man-to-man Judgement

In 2 Timothy 3:16, Paul says, 'All scripture is given by inspiration of God, and is profitable for doctrine, for reproof, for correction, for instruction in righteousness. That the man of God may be perfect, thoroughly furnished unto all good works'. The essence of preaching the gospel is not only to douse humanity in the knowledge of our Lord Jesus, but as you do that, corrections have to be made. Rebukes have to be tendered and instructions must be unleashed. If you see someone walking on a satanic path and do not try to help him retract from it, the Lord would hold you accountable. Sometimes, Christians ignorantly get into activities that do not glorify Jesus. They do things they never intended to do. So, as a preacher or Christian, you have a role to guide others. If you see a sister moving in a satanic path, you have a duty to support her withdrawal out of that demonic route. If you see a brother going against the principles of heaven, you're obliged to help put him on the Christian trajectory. But unfortunately, some Christians are using the slogan 'Judge Not' to justify disobedient actions. Even if you're a Christian, when another Christian corrects you, you must accept as long as you know what you did violates the principles of Christianity. Many would think that when another Christian corrects them, he is trying to prove he is holy or holier than they are. The essence of correction is not to exhibit spiritual supremacy, but to help each other grow and maintain Christian values. The Holy Spirit, sometimes, speaks to you through another Christian. He can provide you counselling by another brother or sister. The Holy Spirit always works in our interest. When He guides you, whether directly or indirectly, it would be to your gain. For instance, if you're supposed to travel to another town by road, the Holy Spirit can send another brother or sister to advise you and impede that journey. This happens many times, when you become insensitive to the voice of the Holy Spirit or when you decide to make your plan inalterable. The Holy Spirit can instruct another Christian to stop your journey and if you obey, the unseen trouble will be revealed and benefit realized. Maybe there was a lethal road accident designed for you and obeying the Holy Spirit would keep you running through a healthy earthly conduit. But sometimes, you decide to be defiant and slowly walk yourself into the snare of Satan. Iniquity has no heavenly impunity. You must make a turn-around from sin. The Almighty God didn't build humanity to swim in iniquity. The Bible clearly defines what happens to disobedient children at the end of life on earth. There are eternal consequences for defying God's commands. When you violate God's instructions, it's the duty of another brother or sister to notify you. That's the first form of judgement man is qualified to execute. He tells you whether what you did is right or wrong. That role of Christians is clearly spelt in Exodus 18:13-16. Moses judged the people of Israel when they had matters. He used the statutes and laws of heaven to guide them. He told them this is right and that is wrong. Where there is no judgement, there would be no amendment. Where there is no correction, misleading instruction survives – people can be easily deceived. Many Christians see this form of judgement as condemnation. From a spiritual perspective, condemnation is a proclamation that your eternal destination is in Satan's domain – When a decision is made that you would spend eternity with Satan. But spiritual correction or spiritual rebuke is not condemnation. In actual sense, it guides you into the Almighty God's eternal domain.

Earthly Penalty Judgement

The other form of judgement is penalty, whilst on earth, when you violate the word of God. The Almighty God unleashes disciplinary packages to disobedient children. In this form, God doesn't put your retribution on hold. He doesn't wait until the end of the world or when you depart the earth. You face the consequences right here – on earth. The Almighty God executes judgement on earth for varied reasons. Firstly, the Almighty God judges man, on Earth, to subdue humanity. He effects judgement to prove His supremacy. When king pharaoh held the children of Israel captive, the Almighty God says, 'Let my people go'. Repeatedly, king pharaoh denied it. The Almighty God executed great judgement on king pharaoh and his fellow countrymen, and redeemed His people, the children of Israel, with an outstretched arm – Exodus 6:6, 12:12-14. God inflicted different plagues, and king pharaoh remained defiant. But when the all-powerful God exterminated the firstborns in Egypt, king pharaoh let His people go. The Almighty God can also execute this form of judgement when He wants to bring man closer to Himself. He judges man when He wants to restore man. In the wilderness, when the children of Israel made a golden idol, a calf, and started worshipping it, the Almighty God exhibited vexation. He slaughtered some of them to restore the bulk of His people. And when Moses pleaded, He warned them to abstain from idolatry and embraced them. God loves humanity. The Almighty God can also carry out judgement when He wants to make a change in man. Saul, also known as Paul, persecuted Christians, especially the servants of God. He was bent on destroying Christian assignments. With passion, Saul did all in his capacity to destroy Christianity. The Almighty God executed judgement on him, by making him blind for a period. But the Almighty God passed that judgement to transform Saul for the benefit of humanity. Paul became one of the greatest Apostles of Jesus. Finally, when man refuses to repent, the Almighty God passes earthly penalty judgement to destroy man. Sodom and Gomorrah offended the Almighty God to an extent that He destroyed them with brimstone and fire. When Jezebel refused to repent of her fornication and idolatry, the Almighty God vowed to destroy her and He did. Jezebel seduced servants of God, causing them to commit fornication and gave them food sacrificed to idols. The Almighty God gave her space to repent. But when she refused, He vowed to destroy her, which He did – Revelation 2:20-23, 2 Kings 9:30-37. Jezebel enjoyed her vices of destroying vulnerable humans, including servants of God. She was continually used by Satan to help destroy Christians. She thought she was powerful, not knowing that demonic success is an eternal failure. The Almighty God executed judgement on Jezebel and Egypt, whilst on Earth. He destroyed them. He offered them penalties right on earth. The God who created man is loving. He loves man so much that He keeps fighting to retrieve man from the hand of Satan. Yes, God loves man, but He loves His word more than man. He doesn't compromise that. When you breach His word, He says 'I Will' and He will. Many see God's love as His weakness. But that seeming weakness transforms into strength, which is demonstrated in His judgement. Remember Jezebel, remember

Pharaoh, remember Egypt. Remember Sodom and Gomorrah, and submit to your creator. This is not to scare you. But to help you remember, that God's judgement is enveloped in His love.

Eternal Judgement

The third and final form of judgement is the determination of your eternal destination. Everyone shall stand before the judgement seat of Christ and give an account of himself –Romans 14:7-12. This judgement is carried out by our Lord Jesus when you face Him after life on earth. The Almighty God is holy and therefore if you want to follow Him, you must be holy. His desire is for man to be perfect as He is perfect. That's why He sent the Holy Spirit – to guide man into perfection. But man, by himself, cannot determine who is perfect or not, except it's revealed by the Almighty God. So, even if you're perfect, humanly you have no power to declare. It's only Jesus who determines who is perfect or not and makes an eternal decision on you – whether you're qualified for heaven or not. But the routes to heaven and hell are clearly revealed in the Scriptures, as the Almighty God wants you to attain a height of perfection. He wants you to strive for excellence. He desires to spend eternity with humanity. So He wants you to make the mark – to get to heaven. When God looks at you, He looks at your decision on sin. He examines your will. The Almighty God wants to see your desire to violate evil. He wants to see a man who doesn't enjoy immorality. He wants to see a man with no passion for iniquity. In your Christian race, when you get to a point at which you think you're perfect, then slowly, you begin to walk out of Christianity. So, continue fighting for excellence. See yourself as someone still striving to make the mark and that serves as the stimulus to get closer to our Lord Jesus. See yourself as a man of resilience, still struggling to make the mark of spiritual distinction. But that shouldn't compromise your faith and confidence. Accept correction. Do not allow Satan to manipulate you – live for Jesus. No man will escape the eternal judgement of our Lord Jesus. Jesus provides us with everything we need to resist Satan, on earth. He presented the Holy Scriptures to man. He sent the Holy Spirit to guide us. He sent the Holy Spirit to empower us. And He is revealing the strategies of Satan.

Two opposing results emerge from the eternal judgement of Christ. These are Condemnation and Commendation.

Commendation vs Condemnation

When you successfully execute your assignment and maintain your salvation, the Almighty God offers you an award. This is referred to as commendation. The Almighty God commends you for a good job on earth. He offers different Christians different awards, depending on their level of performance in their earthly ministry. Some would receive crowns, some would receive 'thank you' messages and others would be received with huge celebrations. But no matter your price tag, if you can crawl into the eternal habitat of the Creator of the universe, then you would live in a vicinity of dignity. The Almighty God has great respect for His word. When He promises a crown for commensurate work, His utterance remains a vow. And He would have no alternative, but to offer a crown for the completed work. On the other hand, when you depart the earth without salvation, you receive a consequence of condemnation. This refers to making a decision that your eternal destination will be with Satan. Condemnation is not like man-to-man judgement. One man cannot condemn another man. There are only two personalities that can condemn you – yourself and our Lord Jesus. Man cannot condemn another man, but man can condemn himself.

Self Condemnation

The only man that can condemn you is you. Sometimes, some Christians accuse others of condemning them, not knowing it's spiritually impossible. A man can condemn your act. He can oppose your earthly action, but no man can condemn you. Only you and our Lord Jesus have the power to condemn you. There are three major ways you can condemn yourself. Firstly, when you reject our Lord Jesus, you condemn yourself. The Scripture says, 'For God so loved the world that He gave His only begotten son, that whosoever believeth in Him should not perish, but have everlasting life,' – John3:16. Verse 18 of John 3 says, 'He that believeth on Him is not condemned: but he that believeth not is condemned already, because he hath not believed in the name of the only begotten Son of God'. When you accept Jesus as Lord of your Life, your creative sin erases. But when you reject Him, the creative sin remains and you perish. That is, you've condemned yourself already. So rejecting Jesus implies self condemnation. Secondly, you condemn yourself when you don't allow the Holy Spirit to reside in you and not submitting to our Lord Jesus. When the Holy Spirit resides in you, you will submit to our Lord Jesus by listening to the counsel of the Holy Spirit and apply what He advises. In other words, not adhering to the counselling of the Holy Spirit implies running into other sins. The Scripture says, in John 3:19, 'And this is the condemnation, that light is come into the world, and men loved darkness rather than light, because their deeds were evil'. When you walk in iniquity, you run into condemnation – you condemn yourself. And finally, you condemn yourself by committing unforgivable sins. When you speak against the Holy Spirit, you condemn yourself. When you blaspheme against the Holy Spirit, you condemn yourself and when you accept the mark of the beast, you condemn yourself.

The Lord's Condemnation

John 3:17 says, 'For God sent not His Son into the world to condemn the world; but that the world through him might be saved'. The physical presence of Jesus on earth radiates salvation. Jesus was crucified because of me and you. He died and resurrected to save us. He presents love to humanity and when you accept His love, He receives you with open arms. But when you fail to receive the commendation of our Lord, you run into His condemnation. When you're not qualified to live in His holy habitat, He convicts you and sends you to a place of eternal suffering. But our Lord Jesus doesn't condemn you without you first condemning yourself. Many times, self condemnation might be hidden. It might be unknown to you, a truth only our Lord Jesus can reveal. The Lord's condemnation is the final condemnation. When God condemns you, you're destroyed. You live infinitely in the domain of darkness, with Satan and his dark angels. Remember John 3:17-18 says, 'For God sent not His Son into the world to condemn the world; but that the world through Him might be saved. He that believeth on Him is not condemned: but he that believeth not is condemned already, for he hath not believed in the name of the only begotten Son of God'. That's why unbelief is Satan's first strategy. When you don't believe, you've condemned yourself already. Jesus doesn't condemn you in this world. You can only be condemned by yourself in this world. Jesus condemns you in eternity, when you face Him on the day of judgement. Our Lord Jesus is the supreme judge of heaven and earth, and so your condemnation must be justified.

The 'Judge Not' slogan should not be used to justify iniquity or any form of satanic activity. Never use it to defend sin. When Jesus talks of 'Judge Not', He cautions Christians to live the word they preach. He warns Christians to be careful to not fall victim to Satan. That's why He says, 'And why beholdest thou the mote that is in thy brother's eye, but considerest not the beam that is in thine own eye?' - Matthew 7:3. Jesus is guiding us to strive for excellence. He inspires us to work harder and keep our Christian garments white. Christianity is like an earthly examination. Servants of God are the teachers. Whether you're a singer, a verbal preacher, a prophet or a writer – you're considered a teacher of the word, as you transmit the gospel of Jesus Christ. But the difference between earthly examination and Christianity is that at the end, both the teacher and student sit for the examination. Even on earth, it sometimes happens where teachers write the same examination with their students – but it's rare. That's why Jesus warns that as you teach, as you correct others, you must guard your own salvation. When you're corrected, as long as it's in line with the principles of Christianity, please accept it. Do not see it as condemnation. No man has the power to condemn another man. It's you and our Lord Jesus that have the power to condemn you. Jesus judges us individually, but the Christian race will not be won by one man. We must work together to succeed in the Great Commission. That's why we must help each other as we go. We must continue to correct each other as we run the race. Generally, humans have weaknesses and it would greatly help when Christians help guard and guide each other. The 'Judge Not' slogan should not be used to protect sin. The only point is that the correction or rebuke should be done with love and humility, not with animosity. But when a brother sees you deviating from the Christian path and corrects you, he loves you. Please accept the correction. We all have the right to correct each other, whether you're a teacher of the word or not. When a Christian corrects another, do not see it as the Christian who corrects, trying to be holier than the other. Christian correction is not about spiritual supremacy. It's about guiding your path into a peaceful eternal destination. Other times, when other Christians unravel revelations received from the Lord, others see it as pride or trying to be too godly. But sharing spiritual experiences helps inspire and keep you in the Christian journey. In fact, rejecting corrections can be regarded as pride.

The 'Judge Not' slogan is cunningly destroying the lives of Christians. It must be eliminated from Christian practices.

Chapter VII

Phoney Prophets

Generally, prophets are regarded as Christians anointed by the Almighty God to carry out His work. They are viewed as chosen vessels who speak the mind of God. In other words, all servants of the Most High God are seen as prophets. But also, there is the office of a prophet, operated by a servant of God gifted to see and speak into the future. However, we would view prophets as in the general sense – all servants of God, and later as specified with regards to the special calling into the office of the prophet. Prophets were considered as highly anointed servants of God. But with the existence of Satan, other prophets are being ordained, which defines another set of the prophetic domain. Satan is tricky! He uses every strategy in his capability to capture the will of man. He does everything within his limited power to deceive humanity. He knows many persons desire healthy relationships with the Almighty God. He is convinced people are yearning to encounter the Almighty God. So, ingeniously, he ordains his preachers to capture the set of mankind who blindly chase a share of the Almighty God's holy meal. Hence, there are true prophets of the Almighty God and there are phoney prophets of Satan.

True Prophets

In the book of Acts, Chapter 1 and Verse 8, Jesus says, 'But ye shall receive power after that the Holy Ghost is come upon you: and ye shall be witnesses unto me both in Jerusalem, and in all Judaea, and in Samaria, and unto the uttermost part of the earth'. The existence of the Holy Spirit in man is not just to guide us in our daily personal life, but to empower us for the ministry as well. The Holy Spirit showers us with wisdom to interpret and preach the word of God to humanity. He empowers us to demonstrate the reality of the power of the Almighty God. When our Lord Jesus was preparing His disciples for the ministry after His resurrection, He instructed them to wait until they were endued with power from on high - Luke 24:49. The disciples lived on earth with Jesus. They walked with Him, ate with Him and prayed with Him. But Jesus says, 'Wait, until you are endued with power'. In the ministry, the principles of heaven have to be followed. The Almighty God can empower you just by a spoken word. But He works through the Holy Spirit to relate with humanity, as our Lord Jesus promises. To do ministry, you need the Holy Spirit. When you speak, demons do not fear you physically. They do not fear your human spirit. They fear the Holy Spirit that resides in you. You might not see Him, but demons know Him, they see Him, they recognise Him. When the vagabond Jews attempted to cast out the demons out of a demon-possessed man, the demons replied, 'Jesus I know, and Paul I know; but who are ye?' – Acts 19:13-18. When demons see a man, they either see the Holy Spirit, his depleted human spirit or a satanic spirit in him. Jesus has an overflow of the Holy Spirit. Paul was full of the Holy Spirit. But those guys who attacked the demons were empty – the Holy Spirit was non-resident in them and so the demons did not fear them. When you're empty, demons do not fear you. And when you attack them, they exhibit repulsive actions to catapult your vulnerable vessel into a destitute status. Every true prophet is full of the Holy Spirit. When the Almighty God assigns you a task, He empowers you to accomplish it. When you speak, heaven endorses. When you work, our Lord Jesus prospers it. When you walk, the Holy Spirit guides your steps. True prophets can either be called by Jesus Himself, or they can call upon Jesus by themselves or through a servant of God, and He answers. Saul had no desire for Christian evangelism. He engaged in obstructing the activities of Christian ministers. But Jesus captured and anointed him for the ministry. David had a burning desire to remain in the presence of the Almighty God. He cried onto God and God replied, 'I have found a man after my heart' – God anointed him.

Phoney Prophets

In 2 Corinthians 11:13-15, Paul states, 'For such are false apostles, deceitful workers, transforming themselves into the apostles of Christ. And no marvel; for Satan himself is transformed into an angel of light. Therefore it is no great thing if his ministers also be transformed as the ministers of righteousness; whose end shall be according to their works'.

Phoney prophets are satanic. They are false prophets. They are prophets unleashed by Satan to help drag souls into his demonic abode. In Samaria, Simon portrayed himself to be a servant of God. He used sorcery and bewitched the people into believing that he was a great man of God, and even the very elect could have been deceived. But Simon was only exposed as a servant of Satan when Philip, full of the Holy Spirit, un-compromisingly preached the gospel of our Lord Jesus in the same city– Acts 8:9-13. Generally, Satan ordains his prophets by two major means. Firstly, he calls them. Satan rambles, searching for available vessels to work with. For some humans, Satan only inflicts trouble on them and for others he just initiates into his kingdom. But for some, he desires to work with them as his recognised agents to actively engage in capturing human souls. And he succeeds for two main reasons; some answer his call because they are empty. As I said, when you're devoid of the Holy Spirit, Satan is wiser than you. He easily captures your will. This set of initiates walk into Satan's trap due to ignorance or satanic vulnerability. Others are ordained willingly. Some join Satan of their own will. The second class of phoney prophets falls within this category. Some phoney prophets were truly called and ordained by our Lord Jesus. But their longing for earthly wealth, supernatural power and other associated physical gains, supported by impatience, walk them into Satan's devilish domain. Their desire for affluence, personal protection and related benefits sink them into trouble. So, phoney prophets are made up of prophets originally ordained by Satan for whatever reason and transformed true prophets who join Satan for earthly wealth, fake supernatural power or other perceived physical gains. When some true prophets see other true prophets performing signs and wonders, they display reactions of envy.

They get distracted from their assignment. They become impatient and their hunger to perform signs and wonders catapults them into satanic nooses. Some phoney prophets influence true prophets for affluence. Some true prophets do not make the required sacrifices but desire an overflow of the heavenly anointing.

True Prophets vs Phoney Prophets

In this contemporary age, it's humanly difficult to distinguish between the operation of the Holy Spirit and the operation of the spirit of Satan. Simon portrayed himself as a great servant of God. When someone portrays himself as somebody else, he tries to do everything the other person does, so you don't detect his stealth. Inhabitants of Samaria followed Simon for so long. They believed in him, as a true prophet of the Almighty God. He succeeded in deceiving them until he had an encounter with the heavenly Anointing. Philip exposed him and his followers realized he was a prophet truly ordained by Satan. Many phoney prophets, if not all, know the word of God – they understand scriptures but do not live by the word of God. Simon deceived residents of Samaria into believing he was a man of God. He was using the word of God to entrap them. He used valid scriptures to initiate the people into the kingdom of darkness. Even his boss, Satan, when he pursued Jesus on earth, employed scriptures. He says, 'If thou be the Son of God, cast thyself down: for it is written, He shall give His angels charge over thee, lest thou dash thy feet against a stone...'and indeed it is written. Phoney prophets can use the same Bible used by true prophets. They can preach the same word preached by true prophets. Satan uses the trick of 'Satan cannot cast out Satan', so that when witch-doctors claim to deliver witches, you would tend to believe they operate with holy anointing and rush to them, thereby initiating you. Phoney prophets use the name of Jesus. They shout the name of Jesus during their sermons. But as opposed to true prophets, they do not refer to the Son of God in their hearts. Whenever you mention the name of Jesus, our Messiah gets attracted. But His action depends on your relationship with Him, or in some cases, He responds to prove a point. So, phoney prophets can profess the name of Jesus, but our Lord Jesus comprehends their intent – He knows they are not true. And nothing happens on the part of the Son of God. But when you hear them proclaim 'Jesus', you may think they refer to the Christ and you might become another satanic convict. Phoney prophets employ satanic powers to deceive humans. When they unleash satanic commands, demons rush into the activities and honour their requests. Unknowingly to many, they glorify Satan. That's one strategy phoney prophets use to deceive humanity, especially those hungry for an encounter with the Almighty God. Phoney prophets perform signs and wonders. They can do supernatural activities that marvel their audience. When Moses instructed Aaron to cast his rod on the ground, as commanded by the Almighty God, to capture the belief of the King of Egypt and let the children of Israel go, the Egyptian magicians duplicated and their rods became serpents, as well. But Moses' serpent swallowed those of the Egyptians – Exodus 7:10-13. Satanic operations are exposed when they collide with the heavenly anointing. They're uncovered when they encounter the Holy Spirit. They are unfolded when revealed by the Holy Spirit. But many times, they operate in regions where the heavenly Anointing is not active. The Holy Spirit is everywhere but only becomes active when you invite Him, or on a specific assignment, as instructed by our Lord Jesus.

When Jesus delivered a demon-possessed blind and dumb man, the Pharisees accused Him of using satanic powers, saying, 'This fellow doth not cast out devils, but by Beelzebub the prince of the devil'. And Jesus replied, 'Every kingdom divided against itself is brought to desolation; and every city or house divided against itself shall not stand: And if Satan cast out Satan, he is divided against himself; how shall then his Kingdom stand?' – Matthew 12:22-29. Jesus defended that Satan cannot cast out Satan. He explains that He operates fully with the spirit of the Almighty God. But in this End-time ministry, Christians have to be vigilant. As I emphasized earlier, when Satan deals with Christians, he knows what to do. Satan manipulates scriptures to confuse baby Christians and continue deceiving Unbelievers. Satan employs Matthew 12:22-29, as another scriptural deception. Yes, indeed, Satan cannot cast out Satan. But Satan is cunning and wicked!!! He produces 'counterfeit miracles' to deceive mankind. And remember, Satan can also punish his agents when they fail on a task or disobey his orders. 'Counterfeit miracles' is a major strategy of Satan to initiate humanity, and hence ordain more phoney prophets. Whenever Unbelievers and many baby Christians see 'miracles', they believe it's the work of the Almighty God. Whenever they see 'healing action', they believe it's a treatment from God. Whenever they see blind eyes open, they believe it's a deliverance of God. Whenever they see people testify of getting jobs, establishing marriages, they rush to get their share of that 'prophetic discharge'. Be careful about who you trust in the ministry. The Bible emphasizes on testing every spirit. Phoney prophets carry out their assignments like true prophets. But phoney prophets do not have the Holy Spirit. That's the major difference between true prophets and phoney prophets. So, all phoney prophets do are enveloped in the strategies of Satan. It's the Holy Spirit that empowers true prophets to overcome the activities of Satan. Satan's operation is encased in deception, but the Holy Spirit uncovers all.

Like true prophets, phoney prophets pray. Prayer is just communication between man and a deity. It's a process of man talking to his deity and the deity reciprocating. Satan is the deity of phoney prophets – he's their god. When they mention god, you might think they're referring to the Almighty God – the great Deity. Similarly, phoney prophets use the name of Jesus to deceive man. It's like someone using fake United States dollars to do business with you. We all know the United States dollar is a universally employed and respected currency. It's used in business transactions worldwide. But only the smart would recognise it's counterfeit. In this context, it's the Holy Spirit that offers you that smartness, as this is a spiritual activity and by your human self, Satan is smarter than you. You need the Holy Spirit. Simon deceived the occupants of Samaria, of him being a man of God. He only got exposed by Philip who's full of the Holy Spirit. Phoney prophets also fast. Fasting is a heavenly principle that enhances the strength of your spiritman. It makes you more sensitive to the Holy Spirit and empowers your human spirit. Remember, Satan was in heaven, so he understands the significance of fasting. When the disciples of Jesus failed to cast out the demons from a demon-possessed man, Jesus says, 'Howbeit this kind goeth not out, but by prayer and fasting' – Matthew 17:21. There's power in fasting and prayer. That's why Satan weakens the spirit of Christians to not pray, and hence not fast. Your prayer living affects your fasting routine. When you don't pray, or pray often, you hardly think about fasting. And slowly, your fasting life dies. Fasting is supposed to be a routine. You need to set at least a day every week to fast. You can fast as a congregation or family, but you must have your fasting schedule. Like true prophets, phoney prophets are also empowered when they fast in relation to their deity. And when you fast, it's supposed to be between you and the Almighty God. But for married spouses, your partner must approve – 1 Corinthians 7:5. And for congregational fasting as well, your fasting schedule will be exposed to each other.

Ministerial pride can transform a true prophet into a phoney prophet. Sometimes, when our Lord Jesus begins to execute great work through some servants of God, they get filled with pride. At some point, they begin to feel it happens by their human strength. They start ignoring the counselling of the Holy Spirit. They stop consulting the Holy Spirit for approval and slowly Satan captures their will. Always recognise the role of the Holy Spirit in your assignment. Always acknowledge that without Jesus you are nothing. See yourself as an impure vessel, purified by our Lord Jesus to be employed for a pure purpose. Phoney prophets can be difficult to recognise, but given below is a guide to help identify them.

Detection of Phoney Prophets

1 John 4:1 says, 'Beloved, believe not every spirit, but try the spirits whether they are of God: because many false prophets are gone out into the world'. Not every spirit is of God. Not all signs and wonders are executed in the name of our Lord Jesus. Not every 'miracle' is of God. Not every healing is by the power of the Holy Spirit. Not every job is provided by God. Not every marriage is ordained by the Almighty God. The Bible says believe not every spirit, but try the spirits whether they are of God. In this contemporary age, making a distinction between true

prophets and phoney prophets is almost impossible. The probability of detecting phoney prophets humanly, is almost zero. However, Satan's strategies can be hidden from man, but it can never be hidden from the Holy Spirit. And as long as you have a healthy relationship with the Holy Spirit, He always reveals Satan's strategies to you. That's why Satan gets mad when you have the Holy Spirit. To fully identify phoney prophets, you need the Holy Spirit. Again, I emphasize the power of fornication. Satan doesn't want humanity to have a healthy relationship with the Holy Spirit. That's why he fights to run and keep you into fornication. He knows your body is the temple of the Holy Spirit. He knows you cannot house the Holy Spirit when you live in fornication and adultery. Every time you get into fornication, you agitate the Holy Spirit and He leaves. Without the Holy Spirit, you cannot detect phoney prophets. To detect phoney prophets, you need the spirit of discernment, which is one of the benefits of having an indwelling of the Holy Spirit. You need to be able to discern fake prophets. When you see or deal with a phoney prophet, you should be able to uncover him. But that only crystallizes when you have the Holy Spirit. To identify phoney prophets, you need to know and understand the word of God. You need to be able to interpret the Scriptures. The Holy Spirit teaches you, as you spend time on God's word when you have Him. When you understand the word of God, you'll understand the operations of a true prophet. You need to monitor their activities and fruits, to see whether they're in keeping with the principles of heaven. You need to scrutinize their doctrine. Phoney prophets can use the same Bible as true prophets. They might use the same scriptures. But if you thoroughly examine their messages, you will find contamination. The true doctrine of Jesus Christ teaches that Jesus is the Son of God. It teaches that Jesus is God. The gospel of Jesus reveals that the Almighty is a Triune God – the Trinity – Father, Son and Holy Spirit. It teaches that you must be born again to see the kingdom of heaven. The true doctrine teaches that the Holy Spirit lives in man and with man. The gospel of Jesus teaches about the operations of the Holy Spirit, which includes tongues and interpretation of tongues, supported by the demonstration of the power of the Almighty God, in signs and wonders, and the working of miracles. The teachings of phoney prophets can be minutely distorted, that in many cases, only the

Holy Spirit can reveal. That's why you must remain spiritually sensitive to the voice of the Holy Spirit, which helps you uncover the strategies of phoney prophets. Finally, you must pray for God's revelation. The Holy Spirit reveals at will, but you must also pray and fast, for spiritual acceleration and sensitivity. Detection of phoney prophets is generally of personal recognition. One man can detect, whilst the other might not. Why? One got the revelation from the Holy Spirit, whilst the other did not. Phoney prophets can be exposed when they encounter the heavenly anointing. This, many times, occurs when they meet with true prophets, as in the case of Simon and Philip in Samaria. When you're able to detect phoney prophets, you'll recognise true prophets.

The Office of the Prophet

The office of the prophet is very essential in Christian ministry. In human existence, satanic activities occur which can only be revealed by the Holy Spirit. Many times, the Holy Spirit reveals through ordained spokespersons of the Almighty God. These spokespersons, otherwise known as prophets, reveal occurrences to humanity, even before they happen. The office of the prophet is so significant that Satan utilizes it thoroughly, to mislead mankind. Satan's prophets can speak and it crystallizes. Their master, Satan, has a relatively weaker power that also operates in the spiritual realm. Regarding future happenings, true prophets speak in three major forms:

Direct Messaging from God – but later revealed to Congregation

The Almighty God reveals to His spokesmen. He unfolds strategies of Satan to guard His Church. He talks to His chosen about the activities of Satan and even about His plan. By this form, He reveals to His prophets, who later relay the messages to His people. The Almighty God can reveal a message today and his prophet reveals it tomorrow. It's not instantaneous. Satan and his phoney prophets do the same, but the difference; phoney prophets operate with satanic powers.

Direct Messaging from God – under the Anointing

True prophets receive messages from the Almighty God, as they are moved by the power of the Holy Spirit. This occurs instantaneously. They speak directly under the unction of the Holy Spirit. In this form, the Almighty God speaks to His people, through His prophet, as the congregation listens. It's not a later revelation. This happens, many times, when the Almighty God wants to transmit an urgent message to His people. Satan does the same to his phoney prophets.

Of their own Will – Endorsed by God

True prophets can also speak of their own will. Remember, when you submit your will to the Almighty God, your will becomes wrapped up in His will. And because true prophets are full of the Holy Spirit, when they speak even future occurrences, heaven validates and their utterance materializes. It might not be a message from God. But, as they walk in His Will, He supports their declarations. That's why true prophets must avoid making a negative declaration against humanity, even when they don't say it meaningfully. For instance, a servant of God can say to somebody 'you'll die tomorrow' and it can come to pass. Satan also endorses the personal declarations of his prophets, but remember, their objective is to deceive and destroy humanity. So all they speak is hidden negatives. Prophets can also speak past and occurring activities.

Effect of Yielding to Phoney Prophets

Physically, a gift from Satan might be seen as a gain, but it's actually an eternal loss. The counterfeit miracles offered by phoney prophets establish satanic covenants. When Satan releases from himself, he expects you to reciprocate. But no matter what Satan offers you, he wants only one thing – a human soul. Satan is wicked!!! He would offer you a car, but he doesn't want a car in return. He would offer you money, but he doesn't want his money back. He can offer you his feeble power, but he doesn't want that power back. No matter what Satan offers, all he wants back is, at least, a soul – he always wants back humans as his compensation. Unknowingly, many enter satanic covenant when they work with phoney prophets. When they give you water to drink, you drink your soul. When they offer you a husband, you marry a demon and might give them a daughter in return. When they offer you a job, you amass satanic wealth and may donate a brother. The only gift Satan appreciates is life – a human soul. So his phoney prophets do all in their limited power to get him exhilarated. Even the phoney prophets, when they fail, Satan doesn't spare them. He punishes them when they violate his orders. So you need to remain careful who lays hand on you. Many people die without fulfilling their destiny. Many depart the earth, not completing their assignments. Why? They made an unknown covenant with Satan. They traded their souls by working with phoney prophets. Many difficulties faced by some, especially Unbelievers, stem from phoney prophets. They enter agreements of temporary 'gain' with phoney prophets and afterwards they get into trouble. For some, their troubles are ancestral. Their preceding parents, or other relations, entered into satanic agreements with phoney prophets. The ancestors are gone, but the covenant was made on the behalf of the existing victims. And until they're delivered by our Lord Jesus, they remain caged. Satanic covenant can be generational – you need to deal with it. Working with phoney prophets can lead to eternal condemnation. When you establish a tie with Satan's prophets, you become part of Satan's team. And being part of Satan's team means you have denounced our Lord Jesus. And if you're not set free from the confinement of Satan, you remain eternally condemned.

Benefits of Working with a True Prophet

When the Almighty God wanted to relate with humanity, He sent His only Son, Jesus, in human form. He did not live with humans just in the spirit. He lived on earth physically. Jesus died, and on the third day, He resurrected. He promised to send us the Holy Spirit, which He did. Now, Jesus is no more living with Christians physically, as He did before His crucifixion. But the Holy Spirit lives with us, and in us. Jesus physically departed the earth, but He is continuously ordaining His servants. True prophets are representatives of the Almighty God on earth. The Almighty God ordains them to work with His people who are ready to relate with Him. Working with true prophets helps cement your relationship with the Almighty God. Every man has access to the Almighty God. Every Christian has access to the throne in heaven. But leadership is vital in every setting. Even in heaven, there is hierarchy and there is order. The Almighty God ordains His prophets to lead the Christian generation on earth. He recognises them as His leading personalities in the body of Christ. They deputize Him on earth. He honours their words and activities. So working with true prophets makes it easier to access the throne of the Trinity. Whenever they call upon God, He grants them an audience and responds appropriately. The Almighty God highly respects His servants. When true prophets introduce you to the Almighty God, it becomes easier to connect. True prophets help you fulfil destiny. They offer you spiritual and physical counselling that guides you into your pre-ordained path. The Holy Spirit is the chief guide to every Christian, but our Lord Jesus uses physical vessels, appointed by Him to help other Christians as they carry out their assigned divine tasks.

True Prophets vs Idolatry

True prophets must be respected, but they're not to be worshipped. They must be honoured, but not idolized. The Almighty God is jealous and never compromises His monotheism. Satan can influence Believers into investing their trust in servants of God, and slowly they get distracted from the God they serve. Some believe that only a particular servant of God should pray, or deal with them. It's not wrong to be loyal to a servant of God. But learn to be open to other true prophets, and your faith should remain in the God of the servant, not in the servant of God. It doesn't mean you shouldn't trust them. That's not what I'm talking about. But as you work with them, you need to focus on the source of their power, which is the Almighty God. That's why every Christian must have a personal relationship with our Lord Jesus because the trouble begins when Christians begin to think that only Christian leaders have access to the throne of the Trinity. The Almighty God highly listens to His servants, but every Christian has access to the throne of the Trinity.

Always remember, phoney prophets are satanic – stay away from them.

Chapter VIII

The Sunday Service

The Sunday service is slowly becoming a satanic platform. Sunday has been set aside by many Christians to converge and commune with their Maker, but Satan struggles to transform it into an altar of demons. Satan opposes any meeting established to glorify our Lord Jesus. The Almighty God likes seeing His followers working together in love. He smiles when His children work in unity. But Satan is cunningly infiltrating holy assemblies to neutralize the effect of heaven. The Almighty God always hungers to talk and meet with His children, but doesn't compromise the principles of His kingdom. In Acts 7:48-50, scripture says 'Howbeit the Most High dwelleth not in temples made with hands; as saith the prophet, heaven is my throne, and earth is my footstool: what house will ye build me? saith the Lord: or what is the place of my rest? Hath not my hand made all these things?' The Almighty God doesn't live in temples built with human hands. Heaven is His throne and earth His footstool, even though the Holy Spirit, which is His spirit, dwells in us. The church building is referred to as 'House of God' because it has been dedicated for carrying out activities of our heavenly Father. It has been dedicated to the ministry. Wherever you decide to talk or meet with the Almighty God becomes an altar – it becomes a place of prayer. The church, I mean the physical structure, has been dedicated for that purpose. It has been designated a house of prayer, where Christians converge to exalt the name of our Lord Jesus. So everywhere dedicated for prayer must remain in keeping with the protocols of heaven. But the contemporary church is slothfully digressing from that purpose, especially on Sunday services, as explained in immediate succeeding sub-sections.

Dress-Coding

When Christians attend church services on Sundays, it's sometimes hard to distinguish between Believers and Unbelievers. Some ladies get attired in enticing clothing that triggers men's arousal for the opposing gender. Application of the word of God must begin in the house of prayer, but if you do otherwise, then what's the essence of attending services? The Almighty God would hold men accountable for not exhibiting continence. Men would be judged for not displaying self-control. They may be held accountable for violating their masculinity. But in the Christian race, Christians must help Christians for Christians to succeed. The Almighty God would also hold you sisters accountable for influencing the fall of a brother. Even the preacher can get distracted. Jezebel seduced the servants of God and the Almighty God destroyed her. Some ladies might be appareled not to deliberately seduce a brother, but in the kingdom of heaven, ignorance is unacceptable. As long as your dress code or action is prone to sin, then you would have to answer to our Lord Jesus. Remember, brothers can also physically entice sisters. During worship or prayer sessions, some members, especially ladies, remain repulsive to the Holy Spirit. When they sense a touch of the Holy Spirit, they remain disconnected as they would not want to fall and mess up their adored clothing. Sometimes, an encounter with our Lord Jesus could be one in a lifetime experience and once you miss it, it never recurs. Our Lord Jesus sometimes shows up with a specific anointing to empower you for a specific assignment and missing it may make your destiny dilapidated. That's why you need to allow the Holy Spirit to do what He wants with you. Pastors and other church leaders should rebuke any member who puts on apparel that supports nudity. Many clothing products are dedicated to Satan – they're designed to exalt the name of Satan. That's why you need to pray on every product you buy, even if it's a three-piece suit. I was invited to a Sunday service sometime ago. The preacher, the head of that ministry, invited a lady and her son, a boy about three years old, to move to the front of the congregation for prayer. The lady's dress was very tight and just below her hips region, way above her knees. Her protruding breasts were partially exposed as if she had just received a proposal for a long awaited romantic date. With her seemingly irresistible attire, she paused just in front of the preacher, who laid hand and prayed for them. She then confidently walked back to her seat, together with her son. Well, I can't tell if the preacher dealt with that situation, earlier or later, but I was expecting an open rebuke or any other form of direct admonition. That could've served as cautioning to other attendees as well. But many times, some pastors and other preachers of assemblies fail to correct members of their congregation regarding dress-coding, for fear of losing members and their associated financial gain. But to lose a member or the monetary gain, which is more detrimental? To lose your soul or the money, which is destructive? To gain a member's soul or the pecuniary reception, which is more crucial? I believe the primary purpose of the ministry is soul-winning. So dress-coding must be taught. Whatever you do in the kingdom of God, think about the effect on others, and not just you. Does your action help protect the salvation of others? If the answer is 'No', you need a rectification.

Church authorities must enforce dress codes for proper service attendance. Some ministries provide wrappings to cover up ladies who expose parts of their bodies that are meant to be hidden. I salute them for that, but the Church needs to preach dress-coding. Remember, that when you pastor or lead a ministry, you would be held accountable for some of the scriptural violations of your congregation, if you don't teach them, even though they would also have to pay. It's good to provide covers, but you need to enforce modesty in the church and help members understand the eternal consequences of satanic coverings. Sunday services are not worldly party appointments. They're not demonic dining halls. Sunday services are not places to showcase what you materially have or what you do not have. They're meant to primarily learn and demonstrate spiritual characteristics. They are meant to learn the word, practise the word, fellowship with brethren and commune with the Almighty God. It doesn't mean you shouldn't dress well, it doesn't mean you shouldn't work with advanced technology, but let heaven be the drive of everything you do – utilize them in the interest of heaven. There's nothing wrong with looking nice, but dress modestly and allow nothing to serve as an obstacle when you're in services. 1

Timothy 2:8-10 says, 'I will therefore that men pray everywhere, lifting holy hands, without wrath and doubting. In like manner also, that women adorn themselves in modest apparel, with shamefacedness and sobriety; not with broided hair, or gold, or pearls, or costly array; But (which becometh women professing godliness) with good works'. Dress decently. Be sober in your dressing. Open up to the Holy Spirit and allow Him to do what He wants to do in you, and with you. When you attend services, your focus must remain hundred percent on our Lord Jesus and related activities in the church service. But if your body is in the church service, your soul at home and your spirit at workplace, then you're truly divided and how would the Trinity work with you? The Trinity is unified and so God likes working with a unified personality.

Technological Distraction

Technology-related distraction is another strategy Satan employs to infect church services. Social media is truly beneficial, but wrong applications are more detrimental than their extinction. Yes, with the period we are living in, you need advanced search devices to do researches, upload and download Christian articles, videos, the holy Bible and other ecclesiastical materials. But do you need to take them to church services? Except on special assignments, but improper use of laptops, tablets, advanced digital phones are supporting Satan's assignment in the church. I was in a church service sometime, and on my left was a young lady, in about a row or two ahead of me. When the man of God referred to scriptures, she would punch her phone and run through the scriptures, as she had a soft copy of the holy Bible. But as she did that, she was alternately switching between the Bible and Facebook. One minute on scripture, the other on social media. And I saw the photographs and communication she was engaged in. How can that attitude help her focus on teachings, not to talk about the application? Briefly, I was distracted from the sermon. But, generally, the Holy Spirit helps me uncover Satan's strategies in the body of Christ. Her action distracted other members, who were around her, as well. In other cases, when people carry laptops to services, they can become obstacles to their encounter with our Lord Jesus. Worship time in services is a time to be focused on the Almighty God. And during that period, the Holy Spirit can do whatever He wants with you. He can make you appear 'drunk', He can put you on the floor, He can get you back on your seat, He can do as He desires. He can anoint you. But remember the Holy Spirit is gentle. He doesn't contravene your will, except on special assignments. So, you have to welcome Him –you have to set the stage for His encounter. But when Christians convey technological devices to services, they normally store them on their seats and during worship sessions, they may not truly focus on the Lord, as they mightn't want to fall and destroy their treasured electronic devices. Why do you need to take laptops, and other related devices, to take notes during church services? What's wrong with carrying a hardcopy Bible? You can use hard books and normal pens, which I believe would be more convenient. And then you can later transfer your info to your devices at home or elsewhere. Learn to not pick up phone calls during services. Avoid mobile phone communications during services. Turn your phones on silent and you would check them later. But the best is to turn them off. Try very hard to make extra appointments that do not clash with your church services. And remember, the best appointment you can ever have is an appointment with our Lord Jesus. Technological distraction is a satanic strategy. But if you believe you can't do without those devices, remain disciplined. Do not use them for extra activities during services, and never allow them to serve as satanic tools during worship sessions. Get them out of the way and enjoy a sweet relationship with the Holy Spirit. But pastors and other spiritual leaders should see if they can set up a place to keep electronic devices for members who carry them, especially during worship sessions.

Skits

Drama is a form of ministry, associated with the movie industry. Plays that transmit the gospel of our Lord Jesus are vital in the ministry. Some understand better when they see and hear information – they best understand audio-visual displays. But we must remain careful to not get worldly practices into the church. When Satan operates, he operates cunningly. Satan can slowly transform Christian plays into activities that glorify him, unnoticed. Some dramas would appear Christian. But when you thoroughly examine them, you see impurities of Satan. In some plays, the Church imitates Unbelievers to explain demonic practices. But if you use worldly dancing styles to do gospel songs, unknowingly you run into the domain of Satan. Children hardly recognise the difference between sacred songs and secular songs of the same musical class. And if you don't help them understand that disparity, they grow up confused and become prone to the strategies of Satan. Even the gospel songs you use, listen to the wording sensitively. But also, parents and guardians should train their children in the pathway of Christianity – immerse them in the word and blood of our Lord Jesus. Then, the Holy Spirit will guide them. Satan can easily manipulate children against their parents and other Christians; so be vigilant.

Pocket Discourse

Unauthorized talking to each other whilst preaching is going on can be distracting, even to the preacher. Preaching time is a period to focus fully on the message. Avoid whispering to a brother or sister during church preaching sessions. Sometimes, you miss a scripture or point and you would want to get it back. But to avoid satanic distraction, you need to wait until after the sermon and make a responsible retrieval from a neighbour. When you try to get a past scripture or point, during a sermon, you would not only distract yourself and others, you can as well miss the current teaching, and continuing in that gets you into more trouble. That's why you need to be closely attentive, to not miss a point. Satan does everything in his power to deprive you of Christian messages.

Pastoral Response

When pastors and other ministers preach, you need to applaud them. I'm not talking about dropping money on the altar during preaching. If you're inspired by the Holy Spirit to do that, it would be good for you, but that's not what I'm talking about. When servants of God dispense holy messages, they desire motivation. The essence of preaching is not to excite you. During preaching, servants of God can prophesy over you and you need to respond positively. So, preaching time is a time of communication. It's not a one-way transmission, just from the preacher. Yes, you have to listen to the preacher, but also, you have to react where necessary. Humanly, preaching is hard. It's exhausting. Servants of God are inspired by the Holy Spirit, who gives them strength. But they are human and need your support to succeed in their assignment. For instance, when they say a good point, you need to clap. When they speak a word over you, say 'Amen', where applicable. During preaching, whatever the Holy Spirit asks you to do, do it.

Sunday Ritual

To some, Sunday service is just a ritual. Some go only to answer to the Sunday register. And outside the church auditorium, they have no interaction with the Almighty God. They only meet or talk with God on Sundays. Sunday is not the only day to attend church meetings and Sunday is not the only day to recognise the Almighty God. Servants of God host revival meetings. They do crusades, which are all different platforms to have an encounter with the Almighty God. The Almighty God is omnipresent – He is everywhere at every time. As I mentioned earlier, wherever you decide to talk with the Almighty God, becomes an altar. So even in your bedroom, you can talk with the Almighty God. In your kitchen, you can dialogue with the Almighty God. At the beach, you can worship the everlasting God. Everywhere you go you can access the Trinity. Everywhere you go, you must remain in touch with the Almighty God. Many times, many people misquote Matthew 18:20. They utter Jesus says, '...where two or three are gathered together, there will I be'. That's not what Jesus says. Jesus says, '...where two or three are gathered together in my name'. He didn't just say, '...where two or three are gathered together'. He says '...in my name...'. He says, 'Where two or three are gathered together in my name, there am I ...'. From the very moment you leave home for Church service, Jesus knows your intent. Some go to get boyfriends, others go for girlfriends. Some go to see friends. Others go because they want to give birth to children. Some others go because they have an appointment to meet with another friend. Our Lord Jesus reads your mind. He sees the heart. And decodes exactly what's in your mind, even before you think. Jesus wants His children to gather together, but He wants them to gather together in His name. So, if your gathering is not of Him, then your Christian association may end up a wasted strive. Whatever you do, the first thing Jesus looks at is your intent – why you do it. You can go to Sunday services for fifty years and have no relationship with Jesus. Someone can attend just one Sunday service and gets an encounter with the Lord. You can be in a meeting where Christians are gathered in the name of Jesus, but if your motive is opposing, you might remain disconnected. Your primary reason for going to Church services should be to have an encounter with the Almighty God, through His word. In a Sunday service, you have to remain focused to commune with our Lord Jesus. The Almighty God loves corporate worship because He says He would be where two or three are gathered together in His name.

The church is a house of prayer, but a Christian ministry has multiple functions. In spite of the Sunday service troubles, there are benefits that go with attendance. Some of them include:

Personal Encounter with God

Sunday service increases the probability of your encounter with the Almighty God. When a true prophet oversees a ministry, the presence of the Almighty God is always with him. When you attend his Sunday service, the stage is already set to get an encounter with the Almighty God and it would only be left with you to connect. Many times, Christians pray to get an encounter with the Lord. Yes, God is Omnipresent – He is everywhere. But as I said, He is not active everywhere. He becomes active when you allow Him or on His special assignment, according to His will. In other words, God shows up in situations when you authorize Him or as He desires. But when His servants preach, it becomes easier to connect to Him, as He is always waiting to respond to their requests. When God anoints His servants for service, He honours their speeches. People yearn for the holy spiritual baptism. Generally, our Lord Jesus baptizes man with His Holy Spirit through His servants. So, Sunday services help you relate with the Trinity easily. I had a personal visual encounter with Jesus. I read the scriptures. I learnt about the Holy Spirit and His baptism. But Jesus used a servant of God to baptize me with His Holy Spirit and instantaneously I prophesied.

Bible Knowledge

True prophets teach the principles of Christianity. During Sunday services, they analyze scriptures which might seem difficult to understand by baby Christians and Unbelievers. Jesus baptizes every Christian with the Holy Spirit. The Holy Spirit lives with us. He resides in us. The Holy Spirit helps us understand the Bible. But the Almighty God anoints His servants specifically to preach His word. He showers them with wisdom, knowledge and understanding to teach others His scriptural revelations. You become spiritually mature when you understand the word of God. The more you understand the word, the deeper you can get into Christianity.

Corporate Worship

The Almighty God is impressed when His children gather together to exalt His holy name. He smiles when we converge to praise and worship Him. He says, 'Where two or three are gathered together in my name, there am I in the midst of them'. When we congregate to worship our Lord Jesus, He becomes active in our midst and quickly responds to the requests of His servants. Some Sunday services should be set aside, just to worship our Lord Jesus. I mean, we should use some Sunday services only to exalt the name of our Lord Jesus through songs, instruments and our own words – nothing more. When we worship our Creator, the windows of heaven become open to us. And when they open, demons flee. And it becomes easier to connect to our heavenly Father.

Service to God

When you worship the Almighty God, especially corporately, He releases specific anointing to specific Christians. This happens many times, during Sunday services when His servants preach. Through that anointing, you are empowered for ministry. The Holy Spirit empowers us to repel Satan. But the Almighty God releases specific anointing for specific assignments. In totality, Sunday services empower Christians for ministry. It also gives you a place in the ministry to offer service to God, even if you don't sense the calling.

Healthy Pairing

Interacting in a Christian atmosphere is sweet – it's humanly beneficial, as well. Sunday services help you meet good old friends and walk you into new bonding. You meet old friends and make new ones. Successful businesses have emerged from Sunday service fellowship. Regarding physical possession, destitute Christians, who walked into Sunday services in poverty, have risen to the heights of business tycoons. Some have become leading politicians. Successful Christian marriages have emanated from Sunday services. You get excellent Christian counselling which helps in building up a fruitful home. 'Drop-outs' have risen to successful professional levels in different career paths as a result of meeting other Christians in Sunday services. The essence of the gospel of our Lord Jesus is not just to preach the word in the spirit, but to see the manifestation in the physical, as we help each other. We engage in the Great Commission. We preach the word. We're heavenly-focused, but we live in this physical world because we're humans. And so we have to meet the physical needs, as well. But remember, scripture says, 'seek ye first the kingdom of God, and His righteousness, and all these things shall be added unto you'. We don't follow Jesus for material gains. But when we follow Him, He takes care of us, as He knows our needs, even before we ask. He is Jehovah Jireh – exhibiting His provisional identity.

Security

Sunday services keep you protected. The Almighty God protects us personally. But also, He covers us through His servants. That's why every Christian should belong to a ministry. Whether you lead or you're led. But you must attach to a ministry. You must have a church assembly you belong to. Many Christians do not understand what their church leaders go through. Servants of God spend hours praying for their congregation. Sometimes, you might be asleep. But they would be awake interceding. As heads, they're the first targets of Satan. When Satan captures the shepherd, the flock scatters. And they become easier to defeat. So many times, servants of God are awake, pulling down satanic strongholds. Sometimes, demons fear you because of your spiritual leader. The anointing is contagious and generational. Abraham's seed is blessed because of his relationship with the Almighty God. Satan flees when we mention the name of Jesus because of the spiritual identity of our Lord Jesus. Synonymously, a servant of God can be so glued to the Almighty God that demons fear whenever they hear his name. Demons would tremble when they hear his voice, and are even afraid to touch his seed or anything related to him.

Many of the contemporary Sunday services have troubles – they are infected. But if we would eliminate those satanic contaminants, then the body of Christ would enjoy the benefits of corporate fellowship.

Chapter IX

Divine Acronyms

Acronyms are compressed forms of expressions, in which every letter represents at least a word in the expressions from which they're formed. Divine acronyms are representations of complete expressions, with spiritual significance. Divinity has to do with the spiritual but does not only talk about holiness. It's not only linked to the Almighty God. So, in terms of divinity, there are holy acronyms and there are demonic acronyms as well. Holy acronyms represent Christian expressions, whilst demonic acronyms signify satanic declarations.

When Jesus was crucified, the divine acronym 'INRI' was boldly printed on His cross. In Latin, INRI represents IĒSUS NAZARĒNUS, RĒX IŪDAEŌRUM (Iesus Nazarenus, Rex Iudaeorum), which translates to 'JESUS OF NAZARETH, KING OF THE JEWS' – John 19:19-20. Unknowingly, Pontius Pilate was inspired by the Almighty God to inscribe that holy acronym on the cross of our Lord Jesus, declaring His earthly identity. But even with that, the identity of Jesus was concealed. Why did Pontius Pilate not write the expression boldly in Latin, Hebrew or Greek, as understood by the people of that time? Satan always fights to hide Christian revelations from humanity. Until His crucifixion, the Jews, Pharisees and related Indigenes never accepted Jesus for who He truly is. But that inscription, INRI, transmitted a signal to them, especially with the strong earth-movement experienced after Jesus yelled and gave up the Ghost on the Cross of Calvary. Holy acronyms can be useful, but when misused, they can be eternally detrimental.

After revealing His identity to His disciples, our Lord Jesus further informed His followers that if any man believes in Him, he will do greater work than He did because He's going to His Father and whatsoever he asks in His name, He will do that the Father may be glorified in the Son –

John 14:12-14. The name of Jesus is full of power. The Scripture further reveals that God has exalted our Lord Jesus and given Him a name that is above every other name and that at the mention of the name of Jesus, every knee shall bow and every tongue shall confess that Jesus is Lord, to the glory of the Father – Philippians 2:9-11. The name of Jesus is the most powerful name ever in existence. Jesus is as powerful as His name. You cannot repel Satan without the name of Jesus. No matter how you pray, no matter how you fast, I don't care how you war, if you do it outside the name of our Lord Jesus, your effort will remain a spiritual injury. Physical weapons only destroy the physical body, but cannot directly affect the soul and spirit. You can command missiles from heaven, you can ask God to send spiritual jets, you can employ different spiritual weapons, but all have to be implemented through the name of Jesus. If you resolve to engage in a satanic contention without the name of Jesus, it would appear as any physical weapon which has nothing to do with the soul and spirit. So you need spiritual weapons enveloped in the name of Jesus, which is the Christian weapon. Jesus always supports His name, wherever it's genuinely mentioned. His name moves with power. The name of Jesus protects Christians from satanic attacks. We find refuge in the name of Jesus. The name of Jesus is our hiding place, but we must acknowledge that your relationship with Him affects the function of His name.

When certain vagabond Jews exorcists attempted to cast out demons out of that demon-possessed man in the name of Jesus, the demons responded, 'Jesus I know, and Paul I know; but who are ye?' The demons overpowered them and they fled – Acts 19:13-18. The name of Jesus did not work for those vagabond Jews, it did not work for those exorcists. Why? They had no healthy relationship with Jesus. Sometimes, Jesus shows up when Unbelievers call upon Him, even though they have no relationship, to prove to them He is their Maker, to draw them closer and to help them believe. But some applications of the name of Jesus are according to gifting, according to assignments. As I mentioned, our Lord Jesus offers specific gifts to specific Christians, as a function of their assignments. He anoints them in keeping with their assignments. So even though we use it generally as Christians, the name of Jesus works according to assignments. For instance, a man with a healing anointing can say to a lame man, 'Arise and walk, in the name of Jesus', and the lame man would walk. But another Christian might say, 'In the name of Jesus, arise and walk', and the lame may not walk. Doing a miracle depends on several factors, which include your faith, the vessel you're dealing with and your relationship with Jesus. But with all that, your assignment plays a great role. It might be that the other Christian whose words the lame man did not respond to is anointed for prophecy or any other gift. So, the name of Jesus works effectively when applied appropriately.

Many times, Christians utter the name of Jesus. But you need to realize the name of Jesus is not only active when you verbally say it. It's also active when you write and think as well. Even in dreams, the name of Jesus can be active. I had a situation in which someone held on to my neck in a dream. I tried opening my speech organ to scream the name of Jesus, but I believe the offender understood my spiritual intent and maintained their temporary satanic captivity. I couldn't physically remove the hand. Suddenly, the Holy Spirit advised me to spell the name of Jesus in my heart. And in my heart and mind, I pronounced 'J-E-S-U-S'. Immediately, the satanic agent released my neck and fled. In another instance, I was attacked in a dream. Someone was holding a machete, trying to cut me into pieces. We engaged in a fierce fight and a knife appeared from a location I couldn't tell, which served as my heavenly defensive device. But the fight was tough, and as we continued, the Holy Spirit whispered it's a spiritual battle. Abruptly, I shouted the name of Jesus and started pleading His blood, releasing the fire of the Holy Ghost. Again, the satanic personality fled and I was safe – they couldn't touch me with the machete. Instantaneously, I woke up praying. As soon as I was up, my wife informed me she noticed me wrestling in my sleep. I normally sleep calm, but that night she viewed my movement, and couldn't decode the reason for that divine tussling. And as she stared, I woke up praying. I didn't just continue sleeping, I stood up and prayed hot for about thirty minutes to repel any further attack and protect my lovely family. It was about 1:00 am. Dreams are real and very essential for human survival, but many times they're treated trivially. Many of the troubles humanity face are initiated in dreams. The Almighty God conveys messages to man through dreams. He encounters man through dreams and unfolds divine instructions to guide and guard humanity. Similarly, Satan communicates with his agents through dreams and initiates destructive encounters with others. He knows many treat dreams pettily and so he uses it as a major spiritual platform to implement his hidden strategies against humanity. Dreams are real! I am not talking about your lifetime goal. I am not referring to your earthly vision. I am not discussing what you want to achieve. I am talking about what happens when you're at sleep. I am talking about when your body becomes temporarily inactive at night. I am talking about what you see or what transpires during your nap or siesta. Many consider a dream as just another sleeping activity. But destinies can be destroyed in dreams and destinies can be made in dreams.

The journey to the redemption of man was established on earth, in a dream. When Joseph walked Mary into his marital home, he misconstrued Mary's conception. He thought Mary had an affair with another man before uniting with him and decided to put her away in secret. That action by Joseph could not have impeded the assignment of our Lord Jesus but could have undermined and might have delayed its crystallization. Mary could have been innocently tagged negative. But the Almighty God who plans and knows everything sent an angel to guide Joseph, as he prepared Jesus for His assignment. Joseph couldn't decode the spiritual relevance of Mary's womb. But the Almighty God revealed the identity and assignment of the unborn baby. Many could have considered that dream as just another activity in sleep and might not have reacted to its revelation. But Joseph, even in that ignorance, believed in the Almighty God and understood the spiritual principles. He had a healthy relationship with the Almighty God and could discern heavenly visitations. When the angel appeared, he knew it was the Almighty God speaking to him – Matthew 1:18-25.

The Almighty God employs dreams to reveal previous, current and future occurrences to help man overcome the strategies of Satan. But unfortunately, when some dream, they ignore or just accept its literal interpretation, with no form of spiritual reaction. Some just treat it as another tiresome event or a recurrence of their daily activities.

When you sleep, your spiritman is always awake – he doesn't sleep. It's your spiritman that communicates with the Almighty God. Satan attacks Christians through dreams. When you're attacked, or you get an encounter, your spiritman responds. But if attacked, the response depends on the intensity and origin of the attack, and the strength of your spiritual stature. You can either repel or concede the offence. Some consider satanic dreams as just nightmares, but they have spiritual significance. The physical is driven by the spiritual. So whatever is successfully carried out in the spiritual would manifest in the physical, except you spiritually deal with it. So remember that the name of Jesus is powerful, even in your dreams. Satan knows that. That's why he fights to obstruct the genuine application of the name of Jesus.

Now, on social media, I see many Christians, including recognised servants of God, employing holy acronyms. Satan influences humanity to employ holy acronyms to conceal the name and related operations of our Lord Jesus. I'm not talking about employing holy acronyms to represent Christian ministries. For instance, using 'LWFOMI' to represent Living Word of Faith Outreach Ministries International. The expression is boldly printed and we all see the corresponding connotation. That's not what I'm talking about. There are many holy acronyms employed by Christians today, but the most outstanding is IJN. Many Christians now use 'IJN' to represent In Jesus' Name. I have seen men of God apply it on Facebook. I have seen Christians use it on WhatsApp. Holy acronyms are being used on other social media platforms. Satan and his agents do not want to hear or see the name of Jesus, especially from a genuine follower of Jesus Christ. Our Lord Jesus commands us to cast out demons in His name. He instructs Christians to carry out the ministry in the name of Jesus. Jesus promises He's going to His Father, and whatever we ask in His name, He'll do it. Satan knows that, so he's struggling to hide the name of Jesus to reduce the power of Christians. When a Christian writes or pronounces the name of Jesus, the activities of Satan are jeopardized in that locality. Avoid using holy acronyms to the best of your try. When you desire to write the name of Jesus, write it in full. Write In Jesus' Name and not 'IJN'. Never use the name of Jesus in the holy acronym. Never abbreviate the name of Jesus. You can translate it into other languages. But let 'Jesus' remains 'Jesus'. Satan can also use 'IJN' to deceive humanity. He's aware many know 'IJN' as an acronym for In Jesus' Name, so he can use it to encode any of his demonic designations. Whether you see it as In Jesus' Name, it doesn't matter. It only helps if you're matured in Christianity. But if you're weak or an Unbeliever, you might easily be entrapped.

Some employ 'IJN' to represent In Jesus' Name because they're ashamed to declare that they're followers of our Lord Jesus. But Jesus emphasizes if you are ashamed of Him in this world, He would be ashamed of you when He comes with His holy angels in the glory of His Father – Mark 8:38. When Jesus is ashamed of you, you would be eternally separated from the Trinity. It's Satan and his followers who conceal their identity and activities to deceive humanity – do not copy satanic tricks! Our Lord Jesus wants the world to know Him. He wants the inhabitants of the earth to proclaim His name. He wants humanity to unravel His true identity. When you want to say the name of Jesus, speak it with confidence. When you want to write it, write it in boldness. When you want to think it, think it in sincerity. Let everyone know you're for Jesus Christ, and heaven would remain proud of your earthly existence. It might sound troublesome, but hiding the identity of our Lord Jesus implies you're teaming with Satan. In other words, you allow Satan to manipulate you, and by so doing, you glorify him. You might not know this, but remember, ignorance is of no excuse in eternity.

Demonic acronyms are used universally. Satan is containing social conversations. In this digital electronics age, people desire to move alongside modernity. Many want to engage in all verbal or written social interactions, whether holy or satanic, they might not know. For this, you would have to excuse me, as I will be running into some slang you may not want to hear or see. Acronyms like LMAO – Laughing My Ass Off/Out, BAMF – Bad Ass Mother Fucker and SMH, which is sometimes modified to SMFH – Shake My Fucking Head. People use them to casually communicate, but they are demonic acronyms. Satan is wicked. He would introduce nice ones like LOL – Laugh Out Loud and would infect some, as previously stated. Satan has so many hidden strategies to capture the will of man. Some might be hard to understand. But the Holy Spirit reveals to set man free from the strategies of Satan.

Satan can use divine acronyms to deceive humanity. He can use holy acronyms employed by Christians, in stealth applications. Consider similar situations. Satan uses words employed by humanity to represent his activities, hidden to mankind. For instance, people know the Arabic word for God is 'Allah'. Satan can use the same word to represent a god loyal to him. But this would not be revealed to his immature followers, except to those who have attained satanic titles – his direct agents. In my Sierra Leonean Mende dialect, the word for God is 'Ngewor' (pronounced 'gay-wor'). Satan can use that word to represent one of his gods, but again his immature/hidden followers will not know of that demonic representation. Synonymously, Satan uses holy acronyms to represent hidden demonic acronyms. In an identical context, Christians use 'IJN' to represent In Jesus' Name. But Satan can use it to mean something else in his kingdom. It doesn't matter how you perceive or interpret it. It doesn't have to be defined by you. It's defined by his agents, his phoney prophets, and when you deal with them, they get you initiated. That's why you need a healthy tie with the Holy Spirit, and hence the spirit of discernment. Many times, Satan employs counterfeits of holy applications. The Almighty God identifies his children with a seal on their foreheads. Satan also tags his children on their foreheads. Satan can employ the same concept of divine acronyms to encode the mark of the beast. He knows humanity is aware of the number of his name – 666, so he can use other strategies to implement his demonic design. I saw an inscription on a material that appeared as three b s – bbb. But when you critically examine it, it's 666. Satan has so many strategies and so in this End-time, Christians have to be vigilant. A Christian identity should not be hidden. Divine acronyms weaken your spirituality. When you get used to them, you become lazy to fully declare Christian expressions. You begin to be less enthusiastic in ecclesiastic practices and slowly you begin to forget Christian principles, including the actual meaning of words. Satan hides his demonic demonstration in holy applications. But a Christian identity should not be hidden.

Avoid divine acronyms as best as you can.

Chapter X

The Chocolate Gospel

The chocolate gospel offers Satan easy access to the will of God's servants. Satan influences true prophets to preach worldly enticing messages. And these messages act as hidden satanic snares to capture the will of Unbelievers and baby Christians. Even matured Christians can be captured. One way servants of God engage in the chocolate gospel is through fundraising.

Fund Raising

Raising money for the ministry can be frustrating. I know how it feels when you have a burning desire for Church growth. I know how you feel when you have a passion for kingdom expansion. I understand the implications when someone desires to see soul-multiplication in the kingdom of God. But you must also remember that the judgement of our Lord Jesus has a set standard. On that day, some would appeal they prophesied in the name of the Lord. Others will protest they cast out demons in the name of Jesus. Some others will argue they did many mighty works in the name of Jesus. And Jesus would reply, 'I never knew you: depart from me, ye that work iniquity' – Matthew 7:22-23. But I long to see all of us celebrate in heaven with our Lord Jesus, after the successful completion of our various assignments on this planet.

Money is essential in earthly ministry. You cannot succeed in worldwide soul-winning without money. But remember, the Almighty God does not compromise His standards. In fundraising, you need to closely follow the principles of the word – evading breaching of the gospel of our Lord

Jesus in other applications. Sometimes, baby Christians might misunderstand genuine fundraising events, and that can sway them away from the gospel. Your objective must remain to attract Unbelievers to Christ and nurture Christians in the ministry. I don't want the rest of humanity to see servants of God as traders of the gospel of our Lord Jesus. You receive the gospel freely. You receive the anointing freely. You must also dispense it freely – Matthew 10:8. Teach the congregation financial principles of heaven, like tithing, seed-multiplication, and let it become a culture. Let them understand that if someone gives $10 and another $100, the difference of their seeds is $90. But when both seeds are multiplied by a factor of 10, the $10 becomes $100 and the $100 becomes $1000. In that case, the difference now becomes $900. So, you see that the more you sow, the more you reap. That's the principle of heavenly-multiplicity. Teach them to understand that the more their seeds, the greater their harvest and let financial prosperity remain a choice. The few minutes you spend on financial teachings during offering time is minute – it's not enough. Yes, for a reminder it's okay. But you can even organize special sessions to teach the congregation on the importance of finance in soul-winning, and hence Church-growth. Help them understand that as Christians, they should have a burning desire to financially support Christian projects. Do not assume they understand, teach them. Members should also not frustrate servants of God – you should not be greedy, you should not allow God's servants to cry for support before helping. But some techniques applied by some ministers in fundraising generate repulsive actions from members who genuinely understand the significance of money in sacred assignments.

I believe in prophecies. I believe in the prophetic gift and the office of the prophet. Yes, the Almighty God can issue specific instructions through a servant of God on financial deposits. And also, a servant of God can issue specific instruction by himself and because he's God's servant, heaven, through the Holy Spirit, can support his pecuniary demand, by translating the spoken words into tangible truth. But when monetary supplication becomes an all-time practice, especially relating to the prophetic, distinguishing between a financial game and a prophetic gain initiates personal mental combat. Heaven might dissociate from such practices and you end up in financial vices. Income generation, in the ministry, can sometimes appear slow. But the God we serve is Jehovah Jireh. When you serve Him in ultimate sincerity, He releases the relevant provision for His work. No matter how long it may seem, He would show up. Do not doubt Him – work in faith. Jesus says, '…Seek ye first the kingdom of God, and His righteousness; and all these things shall be added unto you.' – Matthew 6:33. But when you continue in deformed fundraising practices, Unbelievers and baby Christians might see God as just Jehovah Jireh and would tend to run to Him only because they need material prosperity from Him, and not because He is their Maker. The Scripture warns of the love of money – 1Timothy 6:10. Loving money is a springboard to satanic engagements. The love of money can walk you out of Christianity. The Bible didn't say 'the love of money to fornicate'. It didn't say 'the love of money to commit adultery'. It didn't say 'the love of money to drink alcohol'. It didn't say 'the love of money to bribe'. The Bible says, 'The love of money…so even if you desire to do ministry, when you begin to fall in love with money, you begin to plant, you begin to nurture, you begin to grow satanic seeds. And when you begin to harvest, Satan shows up as the 'chief farmer'. Love your assignment and not the money. Fall in love with your ministry and not with the money of your ministry. When you begin to make finance a god, when you allow money to take first place in your life, that old serpent becomes the master of your life. Teach the congregation about offerings, let them understand the principle of tithing, help them to know the importance of sacrifices and reveal the benefits of alms. Total financial blessing is a full package. You must give offerings, do sacrifices, pay tithes and engage in alms, even outside the church. You must also teach the congregation that giving to the ministry is not just for personal gain. But they should understand that soul-winning must be the desire of every Christian and that when you give, you support missions to win souls, even if you're not physically part of the team, which is eternally beneficial. Soul-winning is the responsibility of every Christian. Ministry is a great sacrifice and I salute you for yielding. But please guard your relationship with our Lord Jesus, and I pray that all of us would celebrate in heaven, with our Lord Jesus after the Great Commission – Matthew 28:16-20.

What then? Is it wrong to be wealthy? Is it a taboo to be rich? Is it not good to be elevated? In 1Timothy 6:9, Paul says, 'But they that will be rich fall into temptation and a snare, and into many foolish and hurtful lusts, which drown men in destruction and perdition'. There is nothing wrong with being wealthy. There is no trouble in being elevated. Your riches only become a curse when you allow its associated temptations to overpower you. When you allow sin to control your wealth, slowly you walk into a satanic domain. Satan doesn't want to see Christians financially prosperous. He doesn't want to see genuine followers of Jesus Christ in control of money because he knows they would invest in soul-winning activities. So, the devil fights against the financial prosperity of Christians. But do not employ satanic means for an earthly ascent. Satan is tricky! As he fights to block the financial prosperity of Christians, he also cunningly uses financial attainment to capture the will of followers of our Lord Jesus. In some cases, he allows some Christians to genuinely make money and as they go, he infiltrates their life with demonic distractions and their financial prosperity drag them into a satanic trajectory. Their monetary gain becomes curses instead of blessings. In other cases, Satan inspires Christians to illegally make money through satanic means – ways that violate the word of the Almighty God. Satan doesn't bother about Believers who make money demonically/unscrupulously – they belong to him, so he's not bothered. Sometimes, that's why you see people who prosper illegally stand on pulpits to declare testimonies of their elevated status. You see employees who steal from their workplaces hold onto a lectern to give testimonies about the stolen gain. A lady doesn't need to sleep with a boss to get elevated. People do not need to sacrifice their relations or loved ones to get rich and tell friends it's the work of God. It's not just in the area of financial growth but other sectors as well, like child-bearing and healing. All these are Satan's strategies to empower man with fake financial prosperity. Satan's aim is not just to make Christians poor or broke. His objective is not just to demonically 'enrich' you. His goal is to steal and destroy your soul.

When Potiphar's wife demanded to sleep with Joseph, Joseph could've destroyed his destiny for a seeming minute's pleasure, by supporting her satanic request. But Joseph understands heavenly principles and knew he was a man of sacred assignment. He knew he had to protect his anointing because he knew his final destination. That's why he thwarted his madam's passion. When Satan sees genuine prosperity, he fights to contaminate it. When the devil recognises heavenly assignments, he struggles to destroy it. Potiphar's wife did not only want to satisfy her sexual desire for Joseph. Satan wanted to use her to destroy Joseph's assignment – Genesis 39. Satan designs systems to devastate the assignments of Christians. Christians must recognise his traps and remain watchful!

When you serve God sincerely, when you work for Him in humility, when you make genuine sacrifices, He blesses you. King Solomon offered a thousand burnt offerings to the Almighty God and God said to Solomon, 'Ask what I shall give thee'. Solomon replied he needs wisdom to rule. The Almighty showered Solomon with wisdom and even riches and honour which Solomon did not even ask for – 1Kings 3. So, there're levels of sacrifices that attract heaven and even if you make no request, God would bless you. There might be delays. But in some cases, our Lord Jesus prepares you for your assignment, and until you're ready, at the right time, He wouldn't let you into it. In other cases, there might be satanic obstructions. That's why a Christian must continually wrestle with powers of darkness. But what does it profit a man if he can gain the whole world and loses his soul? – 1Timothy 6:7.

The Miracle Gospel

The chocolate gospel is not only limited to ministerial fundraising. It operates in the domain of miracles, as well. Sometimes, Unbelievers and baby Christians are enticed by the working of miracles. Generally, life is full of troubles and humanity always searches for the easiest routes to neutralize their effect. Some desire marriages. They want to settle down. They want to build a home they could call their own. Others need jobs. Some others desire to be elevated at their places of employment. And so when they hear servants of God make promises of miracles, they run to them. The Almighty God is the Creator of the universe. I believe in His creative power and I believe in miracles. I believe in the demonstration of the power of the Holy Spirit. But the Almighty God does miracles primarily to win souls. He does it to help Unbelievers believe in Him as the Most High God – their Creator. He carries out miracles to help His people carry out ministry. He does it to destroy the works of Satan. But Satan manipulates servants of God. A lot of people would think Satan cannot manipulate servants of God, but he can when they yield to his satanic stimuli. Satan succeeded in using Jezebel to seduce God's servants. Jezebel served them food sacrificed onto idols and they ingested. I want to believe it's through those food Jezebel succeeded in sleeping with them. Other times, as I said, Satan speaks from the outside and when they yield he manipulates them. That's why servants of God must be highly sensitive to the voice of the Holy Spirit and remain submissive to Him. But sometimes, this happens when they offend God Almighty somewhere and Satan slowly walks into their will. Remember, sin is obedience to Satan or disobedience to God. Sometimes, God gives His servants simple instructions and when they fail to honour them, He gets angry with them. When God instructed Moses to take the rod and speak to the rock, in the presence of the children of Israel, when they cried for water in the wilderness, Moses did otherwise – he struck the rock with the rod. Yes, the water did spring out, but Jehovah was angry and vowed Moses will see the promised land but will not enter it for disobedience, and so it was –Numbers 20:1-12. That was Moses', but God has different ways of dealing with His servants. To some, He would allow Satan to manipulate them when they disobey Him. He will allow Satan to deal with them. So, when Satan begins to manipulate them into preaching the chocolate gospel, it becomes a continued practice and slowly he captures their will and they begin to do what he instructs them to do. They begin to pray for those who are desperate for marriages in exchange for money. They begin to offer prayers for people who need jobs in exchange for money. They begin to receive money from people in exchange for 'miracles'. Grown-ups who want children begin to pay. They begin to perform counterfeit miracles to initiate Unbelievers and baby Christians into the kingdom of

Satan. This chocolate gospel has so many negative effects on people, some of which include the following:

Transforming True Prophets into Phoney Prophets

When true prophets engage in chocolate gospel, they begin to behave like phoney prophets. Generally, Satan cannot control true prophets. So he searches for ways to walk into their will. The chocolate gospel makes it easier for him. Satan knows life is full of troubles and humanity always look for the shortest route to fix their situations. Satan knows man would fall for the chocolate gospel, so he cunningly manipulates true prophets and as they yield, they slowly become his. They begin to give fake prophecies to win humanity. Sometimes, true prophets do so well in the ministry. But when they begin to do extraordinary miracles by the power of the Holy Spirit, they begin to acknowledge self-centred spiritual superiority. Pride walks into them and the Almighty God walks out of their assignment. Satan then walks in and manipulates them into preaching the chocolate gospel. Ministerial pride easily pulls down true prophets.

Idolatry

Man is desperate for miracles. Humanity desires quick solutions to their troubles. And some would do whatever to make them appear successful. When servants of God preach the chocolate gospel, they run into them. God desires to free His children from every form of bondage. The Almighty God is the great Creator of every existing and non-existing entity. He functions as the Trinity – Father, Son and Holy Spirit in unity. He is Alpha and Omega – the beginning and end of everything. The Almighty God has names attributed to His divine personality. Except on special assignments, He becomes what you allow Him to become to you. If you see Him just as Jehovah Jireh, you allow Him as just the God of provision. Idolatry is not only limited to worshipping false gods, or having an unsatisfied passion for an item or event. When you see the

Almighty God in a single name, you see Him as being equal to other gods. He never becomes an idol – God forbid! But, unknowingly, you see Him as an idol. For instance, if you only think you need God to investigate future issues, in other words, prophecies, you see Him only as a 'God of foretelling'. Yes, you can apply the attributes of the Almighty God to specific situations, like Jehovah Rapha when you are dealing with sicknesses. But He wants you to see Him in His fullness. He wants you to see Him as the great 'I AM', who can be anything He wants to become – Exodus 3:13-14. In other words, worship Him whether you're sick or not. Honour Him whether you're happy or not. Come to Him whether you need a child or not. Fast, when you have access to every food. Some time ago, I hosted an occasion at home – the naming ceremony of my second daughter. But the previous day, the Holy Spirit advised me to fast on the day of the event. I wanted to ignore it because I thought it was the voice of Satan, as I wanted to partake of the sumptuous provision. But the Holy Spirit insisted and I yielded. He made me understand why I needed to fast. Going without food for a certain period doesn't bother me, especially when it's a spiritual exercise. But sometimes, you ignore the Holy Spirit and when satanic elements show up, you begin to run into all sorts of spiritual activities. Worship the Almighty God when you think everything is okay. Do not wait until things go bad, because it can be frustrating. The Almighty God is loving . But also, He is a consuming fire – He is a deliverer. When the king pharaoh tried to resist God's will to let go of the children of Israel, the Almighty God revealed His identity as Jehovah and delivered Jacob's children with an outstretched arm. The Almighty God is God Almighty – El Shaddai. But He transforms in specific situations and acts appropriately to reveal His 'I AM' nature. Other gods function in some areas and not in other areas, like the moon god. And even in the areas they function, they are limited. But the Almighty God operates in all areas with no restriction, except by Himself. This is one of the major differences between the Almighty God and other gods. So, as you carry out your assignment, always remember, the Almighty God is the great 'I AM' who can be and do anything and can only be impeded by Himself.

On the other hand, when you yield to the chocolate gospel, you can receive the promise. But Satan manipulates you into extra-caring for the received package to an extent that it becomes an idol. And unknowingly, you walk into Satan's domain. Remember, God is jealous!

Repels People from the Gospel

Sometimes, Unbelievers come to genuinely get an encounter with the true God. They rush into a house of prayer to be a part of the body of Christ. But when they begin to hear the chocolate gospel, they begin to apply their mental strength to decode the spiritual implications. When they see how some servants of God raise funds, they begin to wonder. When servants of God begin to say, 'The Holy Spirit says ten people from the congregation should give $1,000 each', they begin to ask themselves in rhetoric, 'What is this?' When those servants of God begin to harass them for money and other material gains, they get exasperated and no longer desire to know their God. They would say, 'If this is the God these servants of God serve, I don't want to know Him'. They begin to see Christian ministry as a money-making activity. They see Christian discipleship as 'Unbelieving Entrepreneurship'. If they're lost, they would account for not having a relationship with God, but the Almighty God would also hold His affected servants responsible for pushing Unbelievers away from the gospel of our Lord Jesus.

Eternal Separation from The Almighty God

When Satan captures the will of God's servants, when he walks Unbelievers and baby Christians into idolatry, when he pushes people away from the gospel through chocolate revelations, he wins their souls and they become eternally separated from their Maker. This is Satan's ultimate goal – to break the bond between man and his Creator. When Satan succeeds in capturing a soul, he doesn't only gain one soul, it multiplies, as every soul on earth influences other souls in a way, whether positively or negatively. So when one man joins Satan's team, he can inspire other compatriots to join their satanic campaign and it becomes a contagion.

As a Christian, you can help eradicate the chocolate gospel by the following:

Pray for God's Servants

Servants of the Most High God are spiritual leaders in Christianity. They are representations of the Almighty God on earth. They teach other members of the congregation. They guide other Christians, counsel and pray for them. But servants of God also need your prayers. As the Christian team leads, they're the first points of attack by Satan. They are spiritual, but they're human, as well. Therefore, they can be weakened when Satan's attack is intense. As empowered by the Holy Spirit, they have authority to repel Satan. But remember, like corporate worship, there's more power in corporate prayer. An intercession is a powerful tool against Satan. And so when Christians do it together, Satan always loses. Many true prophets who run into the chocolate gospel started very well in the ministry. They preached the true word of the Almighty God. But as they proceeded, Satan attacked in different strategies and slowly they walked into the domain of chocolate gospel. So, as your spiritual leaders pray for you, you must also reciprocate. Do not feel they're more powerful than you and so do not need your prayers. Many times, servants of God go through storms unannounced. They would be fighting with Satan on your behalf, with few hours of sleep. Satan monitors them right around the clock and for little mistakes, he hits at them. Sometimes, they slip, not because of their troubles, but because of your quandary. Every genuine Christian leader will not celebrate during congregational troubles. In some parts of the world, especially in Africa, local pastors get huge unmarried members, struggling to get spouses. Some members harass them to help them get jobs, all through prayer. Others would demand children. In other parts of the globe, members request prayers for other miracles like in cases of humanly incurable diseases. It becomes frustrating when a pastor is amid a congregation with so many problems. And he may have only one option – to pray. Sometimes, pastors pray for their members to an extent that they even forget about themselves. And cunningly, Satan begins to walk into them.

Pay Tithes

Tithing is a command. The Almighty God instructs every Christian to pay at least 10% of his income. And he would bless the remaining at most 90%. You can pay more than 10%, if you so desire, but not less. The essence of paying tithe is to support the work of God. Tithing is meant to run the affairs of Christian ministries. Ministry is a spiritual work but needs your physical support to succeed. The use of money is inevitable in earthly evangelism. But it's very sad to learn that many Christians do not pay tithes. I was on vacation in a certain African country and met with a young lady. Whenever we chatted, I discussed Christian principles with her. She fell in love with my strategy of evangelism and became very interested in my dialogue. Truly, she was hungry for the word and realized I can offer her the truth of the gospel of Jesus Christ. One day, we were seated, talking, and she asked, 'Samuel, I belong to a certain ministry. I tithe, but my pastor spends our church funds lavishly. He spends it in a way I believe is not Christian'. She didn't get into details, but I understood what she was trying to say and she sounded it as a universal view of their membership. She continued, 'I want to start using my tithe to do charity. I want to stop paying tithe to my pastor and begin helping the needy with it. What do you think?' I replied, 'It's good to do charity. It's good to help the destitute. But tithing is a command. It's not a choice – Malachi 3:10. The Almighty God instructs every Christian to pay at least 10% of their income. As long as you belong to that ministry, as long as you have trust in the ministry of that pastor. As long as you believe your pastor functions by the power of the Holy Spirit, you have to continue paying your tithe. Whatever he does with it, he would have to answer to our Lord Jesus. But you have to fulfil your part of the gospel. However, you have another option. If you don't believe in his ministry, you have a choice to move to another ministry. But as long as you remain in his ministry, you must continue tithing to him. She stared right into my eyes, in perplexity, as I unfolded the tithing revelation. I could see it was hard for her, but she believed in me and knew I unleashed the undiluted truth of tithing. There's no point being a member of a ministry in which you don't trust the lead pastor. It might shower you curses, instead of blessings. Because every time he steps on the pulpit, you see a robber instead of a preacher. When he prophesies, you hear a phoney prophet instead of a true prophet. And sometimes, you might accuse him falsely. Other times, you can misunderstand him. There's a class of Christians who feel they pay tithe, but they don't. They only pay a fraction of their tithe and believe they're tithing. I had a friend who was earning at least $1,500 a month. Some time ago, we were together and he took out some money and enveloped $10 equivalent in our local currency – Leones. I asked, 'What's that? He replied 'my tithe'. 'Your monthly tithe?' I asked. He responded, 'yes'. 'Are you playing games with God?' I reacted. He smiled. I rebuked him, advised him and he made a promise to start tithing correctly. Your tithe is only considered a tithe when it's at least 10% of your income. 9.99% of your income is not a tithe – it's an offering or any other form of financial sacrifice in the church. But it's not considered a tithe. And remember, the Bible talks about your income. It didn't say salary. Many Christians think tithing is all about salaries. So they only pay at least 10% of their salaries and ignore other sources of income. The only income you shouldn't pay tithe of is income illegally acquired. When you pay 'tithe' of money received unscrupulously, or satanically, the blessings of tithing transform into curses. You don't play games with the Almighty God. When you pay correct tithes, you make the work of God's servants easier and help eliminate the chocolate gospel.

Offerings and Other Financial Sacrifices

As you desire, offerings should be paid regularly at every church meeting you attend. This helps boost the ministry treasury, as just the tithes may be insufficient. Other financial sacrifices must be made. Financial prosperity in the kingdom goes with financial seed implanted in the kingdom. The Almighty says He would bless the work of your hands. So, you do the work depending on the type of blessing you want. These financial sacrifices are primarily paid in your interest – to raise your financial level, physically. But they help the ministry work to a great extent, as they supplement the offerings.

Support Ministerial Projects

Tithes, offerings and other financial sacrifices might not be enough to fund all ministerial projects. They can be enough to run the day-to-day affairs of the ministry. But when it comes to hosting huge events like crusades and revivals, more funds are needed. The major essence of the ministry is soul-winning. And hosting events like crusades offers an opportunity to a wide range of Unbelievers to get saved. Evangelism is expensive. It involves huge expenditure. It involves travelling, paying for accommodation and other related expenses. So you need to support projects set by God's servants.

Care for Servants of God

Servants of God are human. They eat the word of God. But they also eat bread. They eat the rice you eat. They drink the water you drink. They drink the juice you drink. They need to be refreshed. They wear clothes. So they need to be well taken care of. Yes, they are supposed to get allowances from the tithes and offerings you pay. But to help save them from eternal trouble, you need to support them financially. They work for the Almighty God. But as I said, God doesn't compromise His judgemental principles. If they spend ministry funds inappropriately, God offers them commensurate penalties. So take care of your spiritual leaders and don't drive them to interfere with the ministry finances.

Advise them

Pray for the servants of God, but you must also advise them. Advice does not necessarily have to be confrontational. If you can, fine, but you don't need to meet them in person. You can do it through other spiritual leaders they talk with. You can do it through their spouses, relations or close friends. You can do it on social media. As I said, servants of God are human. Before they got saved, they had weaknesses. As Christians, the Holy Spirit empowers them to overcome those weaknesses. But as I revealed earlier, Satan uses your weakness to pull you down. So even as spiritual leaders, Satan fights to pull them down through their weaknesses. And some of them might be slowly walking into their weaknesses without their recognition. So as you pray for them, advise them. Do not gossip about them, as the chocolate gospel is eternally destructive.

When a servant of God derives financial proceeds through the chocolate gospel, he may feel anointed. When the congregation generates physical gains via chocolate gospel, they celebrate. Chocolate appears delicious. When you eat it, it feels sweet. It feels tasty. But when you get excess of it, the reactions begin to show up. You can cultivate a tooth cavity. You can run. You can develop rashes/itches on your skin. And in extreme cases, you can be diabetic, which could lead to your extermination. Like chocolate, the chocolate gospel appears rosy, but as you go, you run into random vices and its detrimental effects begin to show up. You may end up destroying your soul.

Avoid the chocolate gospel. It can be eternally damaging.

Chapter XI

The Spirit of Unforgiveness

When a man is infected with a tapeworm, it feeds from him. Parasitically, the worm eats from the beneficial part of the man's digested food. And when it continues living in him, the side effects begin to show up. He begins to feel hungry shortly after eating. He starts losing weight. This can be due to ignorance, negligence or lack of appropriate medication. When a man doesn't know of the existence of the tapeworm, he doesn't even think about it. In other cases, he knows the worm exists, but is not aware he carries it. In some cases, a man knows he carries it, but doesn't make the required effort to get rid of it. And sometimes, you know, but unavailability of appropriate medication for whatever reason promotes its existence. When Satan fails to entrap you through his enticing activities, he cunningly drops hidden deposits into you. Our Lord Jesus says, 'Blessed are the pure in heart, for they shall see God' – Matthew 5:8. Spiritually, seeing God can be viewed from two different perspectives. The first occurs in time domain – on earth, when you get an encounter with Him. In this context, I am referring to the visual encounter – when you see Jesus. The second occurs in eternity. But this one talks about living with the Almighty God. Because even people who die and go to hell can see Jesus, as He is in control of every existing entity. But the condemned in hell do not have access to the Almighty God, as they don't reside with Him in heaven.

One of the most, if not the most difficult practices in Christianity is forgiveness. When someone hurts you intensely and you have to swallow it, when someone callously treats you and you have to let it go. When a friend tries to pull you down and you have to embrace him, these are not tasks many can accomplish. But like the tapeworm, unforgiveness secretly eats you up and you become spiritually lean.

Sometimes, you know and do something about it. Sometimes, you know and don't do something about it. Other times you don't know and so you do nothing about it. In other cases, you know and would want to do something about it, but you couldn't due to other resisting reasons. Many times, people fight with the heavenly revelations. When somebody says he gets a visual encounter with our Lord Jesus, the spirit of unbelief takes over and they oppose. Sometimes, Christians pray to get a visual encounter with our Lord Jesus, but you cannot get that encounter with Him when your heart is impure, except on His special assignment. The Almighty God cares about the state of your heart. Jesus says, 'Blessed are the pure in heart, for they shall see God'. You can have the Holy Spirit, but if your heart is impure, your relationship would not be healthy. And remember, the link between man and the Trinity is the Holy Spirit. Our Lord Jesus speaks to us through the Holy Spirit. So if the Holy Spirit is not happy with the state of your heart, He would not connect you to the Trinity. Unforgiveness is a satanic deposit in man. When Satan recognises you have a healthy relationship with the Almighty God, he searches for ways to disconnect you from heaven. Sometimes when the Holy Spirit speaks, you find it difficult to decode, as Satan speaks simultaneously. And because you're on a different frequency with heaven, you cannot distinguish between the voice of God and the voice of Satan. When you're hurt, Satan triggers the spirit of unforgiveness in you. And he would continue deceiving you that you still have a healthy relationship with God. But the Holy Spirit always speaks. He always reveals our spiritual status – that's the luxury of having Him.

Forgiveness, sometimes, goes with consequences. If I give you ten cups of rice for safe keeping and when I demand it, you tell me four cups are missing. I give you for the second time and you tell me the same thing on request. I would stop giving you for safekeeping to protect our relationship. If every time you get into my bedroom something gets missing, I'll put your entry on hold. I wouldn't hold it against you, but until I verify your integrity, your trust would remain suspended. Forgiveness is one thing, but trust is another. When Jesus cast out all that sold and bought in the house of God and overthrew the tables of the moneychangers, He rebuked them, corrected them, but did not say

'Okay, bring back your tables in, I have forgiven you' – Matthew 21:12-13. Jesus disciplined them and ministered to the people afterwards. That's why there are consequences for ill-actions. But unforgiveness destroys your relationship with the Holy Spirit. The Holy Spirit can be in you, but His counselling would drown in your unforgiveness. And so, you would struggle to make heavenly decisions – actions supported by our Lord Jesus. When you pray, you would find it hard to hear from the Almighty God, as there would be a partial spiritual barrier established by your unforgiving lining. Satan cannot control a Christian – I mean a true follower of Jesus. Satan can only manipulate you when you offer him your will. So, when you allow unforgiveness in your heart, you plant a satanic seed in you.

There are many ways Christians and Unbelievers, unknowingly accommodate and nurture unforgiving seeds within. For instance, if a waiter in a particular restaurant, speaks to you recklessly and you decide to not patronise him anymore, you're beginning to fertilise an unforgiving seed. If you get an issue with someone and the issue is physically resolved, but every time you see him, you look to another direction, you're germinating unforgiving seed. Reminiscence is not synonymous to unforgiveness. It's natural to recall an incident transpired between you and someone when you see him. But it only becomes trouble when you decide to use it as a revenging tool. Matured Christians can handle those situations professionally, but baby Christians might easily nurture the unforgiving seed. Does forgiveness impede you from being angry? When the moneychangers and their counterparts made merchandise of the house of God, our Lord Jesus threw out their trading. He rebuked them, but afterwards, the same Jesus preached His gospel to the same people He rebuked. When you're hurt in whatever way, your anger might show up. But Jesus teaches us that anger and rebuke must be succeeded by correction and hence, reconciliation on the genuine matter. What then? Am I promoting anger? No! I'm unfolding the reality of humanity. Generally, anger is a reflex action. It's a reaction to an offensive action. It's sometimes difficult to preclude, but the good news is, you can control it. So, when your anger is triggered, fight to contain it within your domain.

David understood the importance of a pure heart, that's why he cried onto the Father to create in him a clean heart and renew a right spirit within him – Psalms 51:10. Do not cultivate an unforgiving tree in your heart and allow the Almighty God to get an everlasting one-on-one encounter with you.

Effects of Unforgiveness

Unforgiveness makes you bitter. Many times, when you're hurt, it becomes difficult to swallow. It appears as a bitter pill. You try to push it down, but it fights to remain in the throat. You continue living with it and it becomes your best friend. When it becomes your best friend, it wouldn't want to leave you anymore. Consequently, the healthy relationship between you and the Holy Spirit begins to evaporate. There are two major sources of unforgiveness. These are Direct Source and Indirect Source.

Direct source of unforgiveness refers to when someone hurts you directly. When someone physically slaps you in the face and you can't reciprocate, it becomes difficult to eat. When a superior maltreats you and you have no power to defend yourself, you keep it. When someone of higher status in society violates your human rights and you couldn't let justice prevail, you plant it in your heart. Sometimes, even when you reply, you hold it. This germinates into an unforgiving tree.

Indirect source talks about when someone related to you like your son, daughter, parents or just a friend is hurt. You empathise with the victim. You see the situation as if it were yours. You take up the offence and personalise it. Sometimes, your relation or friend could be responsible for their trouble, but because they're related to you, you support them, even if you acknowledge they're at fault. Sometimes, people are directly hurt as a result of their misconduct. They do something erroneous and they get hurt by someone in return. Some get wounded for doing the right thing due to an interpersonal feud. Other times, people get hurt and they don't know the cause. The same applies to indirect sources. Your relation or friend can be hurt and you don't know the cause, but you support him and nurture an unforgiving seed. The effect of unforgiveness is always negative. There's no positive side of unforgiveness. Unforgiveness leads to the following:

Affects your relationship with Others

When you live with unforgiveness, it affects your relationship with others. You get easily irritated. And you respond negatively, not because of the current situation that befalls you, but because of the unforgiving seed you live with. Always, you get issues with others because whenever they speak against anything you do, they trigger your unforgiving circuit.

Can destroy your Destiny

Unforgiveness can destroy your destiny. When you have issues with other people, some can fight to retard or preclude your progress. Some who are supposed to help you grow can turn against you. But even the sponsors who refuse to support you due to unforgiveness can lose. You might be someone with great talent and assignment that can transform humanity or do something which they, the supposed sponsors, can personally gain from. But unforgiveness can deprive them of that future benefit. Your reason for existing is to carry out your assignment. When your destiny is destroyed, you cannot fulfil your assignment and your existence becomes unserviceable to heaven and to humanity.

Can lead to untimely death

Unforgiveness is not only limited to the probability of destroying your destiny; it can also support your extermination. For some people, when you have issues with them, they limit it to earthly persecution. But for others, they fight to prematurely capture your life and send you to eternity. Many do not believe in untimely death. But you can be cut off by yourself or someone else, when you live in unforgiveness.

Affects your relationship with the Holy Spirit

The Holy Spirit is a loving personality. The Holy Spirit likes working in an atmosphere of love, peace and unity. When you accommodate detestation in your heart, you offend the Holy Spirit. His counselling ceases with time. And if not fixed, He can leave.

Cultivates a Healthy Platform for Sin

Unforgiveness breeds sins of different categories. It's a fertile locality for iniquity. When someone hurts you and you refuse to let it go, you develop hate for him. You lie against him. Whenever he does something successfully, you get jealous, as you would wish nothing positive to happen to him. In extreme cases, you seek to diminish his lifespan.

Personal/Self Unforgiveness

Many do not know they can exist in personal unforgiveness. In other words, you do something and you don't forgive yourself. That's a terrible state! You get into a deal that ends up negative and you don't forgive yourself for entering into it. You get into an illegal business and you're defrauded. You get into a genuine business and you're duped. You get bitter. You consider all lost. You make a satanic covenant and cannot reverse it. You get frustrated and you believe there is nowhere else to run to. Sometimes nobody knows, save you and the Almighty God. But it keeps eating you up and you believe the best option would be to leave the earth. You decide to depart the earth by committing suicide. Many of the suicidal cases are due to personal unforgiveness. This is a strategy of Satan to add to his deceived deceased. You think you would find peace when you eliminate yourself from the planetary fight. But the worst happens when you face our Lord Jesus. You need to understand that suicide is self-murder. As you can be charged on earth, you can also be charged and convicted in eternity.

Unforgiveness vs Sin of the Mind

Unforgiveness is a sin of the mind but breeds physical sins. It's human to host grief when you're hurt by someone, whether directly or indirectly. You develop hate and continually nurture unforgiving seeds. Like faith, unforgiveness can be like a mustard seed. It begins small but grows into a huge tree. And at that point, you become so wounded that you desire the worst to happen to your offender. Other sins of different categories rush in – lying, cheating, etc. Someone can even fight to sleep with your spouse/relation just to hurt you as a result of unforgiveness. So you see that unforgiveness can even lead to fornication/adultery. Unforgiveness is satanic and when it's matured, only our Lord Jesus can deliver you.

Unforgiveness vs Racial Segregation

Unknown to many, Satan employs racial discrimination to set humanity apart. He uses racial fights to divide mankind. The Almighty God desires to see humanity work in love. But man cannot work in love when man is divided. Satan walks in with situations that lead to racial conflicts. He sets humanity against each other and when they collide, he sits back and enjoys man killing man. George Floyd, a black man who was undergoing spiritual transformation, was murdered in cold blood by a white man, a Minneapolis police officer, in Minnesota, United States. George begged for his life. He struggled to sustain his breathing. He fought to not depart this world unprepared, but the police wouldn't listen. The autopsy/necropsy carried out by an independent pathologist revealed Floyd died of asphyxia. He was deprived of oxygen. He got suffocated and became unconscious, after crying 'I can't breathe'. He was rushed to the hospital, where he breathed his last breath. As George was on the ground gasping for oxygen, he cried for help to his biological incubating machine. He called upon his deceased mother who passed away two years ago, as reported, exactly from the date he also departed. When you hear or see a grown man, of about forty-six, calling upon his deceased mother for help, it explains the level of unbearable torture. And their coincidental deaths would continue to re-echo compassionate memories in the ears of loved ones and all in love with humanity. I have seen videos, heard reports and witnessed scenes in which police officers treated suspects inhumanly. But a suspect is not a criminal. A suspect remains a suspect until proven otherwise. A suspect remains innocent until found guilty. A suspect remains not guilty until convicted. And only the judiciary, the court, has the power to make that judgement. Treating a suspect as a criminal is a constitutional breach. It's a human rights violation. Only the court has the adjudication to pass that ruling. Even if a suspect refuses arrest, force should only be employed to get him handcuffed and not to brutally assault his human right. From media reports, George Floyd allegedly presented a fake $20 bill in a supermarket or restaurant to get some stuff. And the police were called. But that was an allegation and was supposed to remain an alleged case, until judgement was made by the court. So, whatever George might have done wrong could never be used as a justification for his humiliating extermination. His family was wounded. They would miss him. Friends would miss him. The world would keep remembering him. Man becomes bitter against man and the spirit of unforgiveness crawls in. The Almighty God instructs man to win souls. The objective of the gospel of our Lord Jesus is to win souls and so, forceful human extermination of any form remains outrageous. It is unacceptable. For whatever reason, no man should take the life of another man. And we must acknowledge the fact that a black Christian is a Christian. A white Christian is a Christian. There is no racial segregation in heaven. There is no racial segregation in hell. There is no colour discrimination in eternity. There is no special place for Blacks. There's no peculiar habitation for the Whiteman in eternity. The Almighty God sees man as man. The police officers offended the people. They hurt the global Black community. But I was so moved when I saw white protesters amid Blacks, which depicted it was not just about George Floyd. You could see different races prostrated on the ground, in the open, in George Floyd's dying position, as he was handcuffed. It was not just about America. It was not just about the Blacks. It was about humanity. The Minneapolis police officers did hurt the people of the world. There were protests in different parts of the world – like the U.K. You could see widespread looting, perpetrated by different races, in expressions of anger and dissatisfaction of the George Floyd murder in the United States. Some might have used that opportunity to replenish their kitchen shelves, especially when the COVID-19 economic trouble wave swept the world. They lost care about the devastating effect of the corona virus. But no matter the case, the Minneapolis police force, represented by a murderer, were responsible for the hardly controlled protest. But even if George Floyd was a white man, murdered by a white or even a black police officer, I expect peaceful protests regarding desired justice. Again, no man has the right to take away the life of another man. No man has the authority to condemn another man. Whosoever does that must face the jurisdiction. The only consequence I'm opposed to is the death penalty, because as I said, no man has the authority to terminate the life of another man. The 'an eye for an eye law', preached by Moses, should no longer be in existence. Jesus preaches forgiveness, wrapped up in love. George was allegedly arrested for a $20 bill case. But thousands of dollars were lost during the looting. Yes, the law has to be applied, even for a penny. But it also explains your reaction to every action is highly significant and must be discharged with wisdom. However, I was thrilled when I saw the police display professionalism in Minneapolis. Protesters made advances to put up a fight against them. But to the greatest shock, the police officers all knelt , begging for mercy. I was moved with sentiment. And I employed my masculinity to resist a feminist tearing. Satan uses situations, especially of a global nature like that of George Floyd, to cultivate unforgiving seeds in the hearts of humanity. When we are divided, it's a plus to Satan. I call on the family of George Floyd to let go. I call on friends of Floyd to let go. I call on the global Black community to let go. I call on the world to let go of any hate relating to George Floyd's murder. I know the world would always remember him. But an unforgiving seed is satanic. It destroys humanity. From other social media sources, I realized George Floyd and the police officer Derek Chauvin, who murdered him, both worked in a nightclub at Minneapolis. There were unconfirmed sources, supported by photographs, that George Floyd was very popular, especially among the ladies, even the white. They likely had an interpersonal feud, for whatever reason. You could see that the way Chauvin knelt on George was abnormal, especially on someone he knew. His action was callous! That's one of the troubles of unforgiveness. When you hold something against someone, you develop hate. You cultivate jealousy. You sow envy. You might always want the worst to happen to him, even if it involves trading his soul. But you might do it and later run into an everlasting regret. That's why you shouldn't accommodate unforgiveness. As part of his transformation, I was moved with sentiment when I learnt how George just started supporting evangelism in Minneapolis, Minnesota.

The death of George Floyd revealed two major facts: the Blacks were unfairly treated and racial unforgiveness existed. For too long, the African-Americans cried in the dark, because they walked in the open, but were not seen. They screamed and they were not heard. They were shot in the chest, with no justice served. They protested, but they were rejected. They appealed and they were repealed. But the verdict of the George Floyd murder depicts that Black people have been seen. The conviction of the murderer was evidence that the African-Americans have been heard. The Floyd tears, after the verdict, were a symbol of a prolonged victory. Silence is not peace. The African-Americans were silent, but they were bitter. They were full of hate. They were full of resentment for the unfair treatment, which only ignited when George cried, 'I can't breathe'. Floyd's neck was pinned to the ground. And we all saw the results. The consequence of hosting grudges is destructive. It's devastating. That's why when there's an issue, speak it up and settle it as soon as possible. Humanity is one and must remain one. Apartheid should not be accommodated. Racial Injustice should not be nurtured. It's a killer! You could see the love displayed for George even from his funeral casket. But it was not just about Floyd, it was about the African-American race. It was about the Black community. The world should be talking more about the human race, rather than black and white races. Yes, like our traditional/cultural origin, we all belong to different colour origins, but all races must remain equally respected. We should live in a unified global Christian society. But Satan always promotes animosity among humanity. The devil never wants to see unanimity among humanity. He searches for a minute springboard. But when every man sees every man as a brother, when every man sees every woman as a sister, when every man sees every man as a friend, the world would get a smooth sail and there would be no place for Satan. Even in the church, racial fight exists and Christians must understand that any form of unfair treatment among humanity is satanic. The answer is brotherly love, Agape Love.

Righteous Anger

Some hide under the hood of righteous anger. They hurt people and tag it 'Righteous Anger'. Jesus got angry for the violation of the principles of Christianity, but His reaction was succeeded by disciplinary actions – rebuke, correction and reconciliation. Jesus taught the people how to do it right. The principle of righteous anger, many times, is wrongly applied by Christians. Do not use that quote to transmit unjustified anger – it breeds unforgiveness.

Dealing with Unforgiveness

Given is a guide to dealing with unforgiveness:

Investigate the cause of trouble
Sometimes, people host grief for the wrong reasons. Whenever there is a situation, try to investigate and know the true cause. Unverified detective assumptions can be disastrous. Prove the suspect's information before reacting.

Pray
Unforgiveness can be hereditary. But Satan uses it to capture the will of man. Satan is a spiritual being. So the only way you can repel his attacks is by praying. Unforgiveness is satanic. It's a satanic spirit. You need to pray against it. David asked the Almighty God to create in him a clean heart and renew a right spirit within him. David tried to have a healthy heart by himself. But at some point, he realized it was spiritual. He realized he needed help from the Almighty God. He acknowledged the importance of the Holy Spirit in that regard. To maintain a healthy

heart/mind, you need the Holy Spirit. Your mind will only remain free of satanic impurities when you have the Holy Spirit.

Application of Scripture

Many run into troubles, leading to unforgiveness by misconstruing scriptures. They misunderstand the word of God and so, apply it wrongly. The Scripture says, 'Whoever is angry with his brother without a cause…'.For this scripture, some treat their offenders cruelly. It's good to apply disciplinary actions. But after that, there must be reconciliation. Firstly, you need to understand that anger is not identical to unforgiveness. Jesus got angry when the temple was turned into a marketplace. He got angry with the people but did not hold grief against them. He rebuked them, threw their stuff away and taught them what to do. He did not house unforgiveness. Jesus gets angry when you violate the principles of Christianity. Whenever you breach the word of God, Jesus sees it as glorifying Satan. He sees it as a gain to Satan. Remember, sin is disobedience to God. Sin is obedience to Satan.

Listen to the Holy Spirit

Whenever you go wrong against God, the Holy Spirit notifies you. Whenever you want to go wrong against our Lord Jesus, the Holy Spirit cautions you. He advises you on the right route. He warns you of the previous, present and emerging troubles. When you want to sow an unforgiving seed, the Holy Spirit cautions you. But many do not listen to His counselling, especially when they want to satisfy their unsatisfied passion. When you honour the utterance of the Holy Spirit, you don't plant unforgiving seeds.

Counselling

The Holy Spirit is our Chief Counsellor. But there are human counsellors, as well. There are professional counsellors and there are counsellors ordained by the Almighty God, like church elders. They speak into you. They settle disputes. They help you relieve internal stress. Sometimes, you become wounded and difficult to forgive. But professional counsellors and ordained spiritual elders of the church can help revive your bitter inner man. Moses had a commission to settle scores among the children of Israel.

Say it
When you have an issue, saying it can help you out. When you let an offence off your chest, it becomes easier to forgive. It's a relief. There are many ways you can say it. Some speak it orally. Others write it. Some others sing it. Some act it. For me, one of the ways I relieve myself of offences is by writing. Writing is cathartic. Writing is an emotional relief. There are some issues, until you write them, they remain in you.

Face the Other Party
There are cases in which you don't just say it, but you need to face the other party involved. In doing this, you have to be cautious. You need to verify you would be welcome. This is to prevent further trouble. Sometimes, people you offend might still hold grief against you. Other times, people who offend you might still hold it against you. So you need to ensure protection for a safe dialogue. Talk with the offender or offended and let them realize their faults. Sometimes they are unaware. Sometimes they do not know it's wrong. But when you talk with them, they realize their errors. Sometimes all they need is counselling. Some even cry, to get it off their chests.

Let it go
All the other guiding principles help eliminate unforgiveness. But the ultimate goal is to let it go. The Holy Spirit guides you. He is our chief counsellor. Spiritual leaders can counsel you. Professional counsellors can speak to you. But you have the choice to keep it or let it go. Allow the hurt to go. No matter what transpires, let it go. Your eternity is very essential. Infinitely, you live there and so you need to secure a safe place in eternity.

Radiate Love
When you walk in love, you don't accommodate unforgiveness. You don't nurture hate. You don't house grief. You don't support resentment. The Scripture says, 'Love your neighbour as thyself'. If you

love someone, all you want for him is peace. All you desire for him is happiness. All you would wish him is true success. Radiate love to every man – not just your friend or relation. Remember, God is love. If you love God, you must also love 'Love'.

Chapter XII

Slandering

Words, whether spoken or written, transmit power. Words define you. Words define others. Words define situations. The holy Bible envelopes written words employed to save humanity. The world was created by the Almighty God through spoken words. In the beginning, God says, 'Let there be...'. Words have life –they can live forever. Satan believes in the authority of words. That's why when you shout 'In the name of Jesus', the devil trembles and flees. In Matthew 21:21-22, Jesus says, '...if ye shall say unto this mountain, be thou removed, and be thou cast into the sea; it shall be done'. The Almighty God empowers your words through the Holy Spirit, so whenever you speak or write, your words move with authority. Satan duplicates heavenly elements. The Almighty God employs words to solidify His spiritual intent. Christians employ words empowered by the Holy Spirit to do ministry. Similarly, Satan, his dark angels and human agents employ words to entice humanity into their lethal territory.

Death and life are in the power of the tongue – Proverbs 18:21. The Almighty God empowers our words to glorify Him. But the same tongue that makes has the power to break. The same tongue that builds has the power to destroy. As Satan fights to entrap you with unforgiveness and other sins of the mind, he employs other hidden strategies to enforce scriptural violations. And one of the major ways is unleashing the spirit of slander. Being talkative can be hereditary – it can be human. But slandering is satanic. The chief dark angel, Satan, uses slander to carry out his demonic assignment. Satan engages Christians in slander and they find it difficult to recognise its demonic implications. Satan uses the tongue of man to proclaim and execute death instead of life. He uses the human tongue to pull down the works of Christianity. Slander is satanic! In our age, some Christians are sometimes scared to share some experiences with other Christians, as before you know it, it becomes more popular than a Sunday sermon. People share their private issues with others, sometimes to help in the form of counselling or other forms of support, and before you know, it spreads faster than diffused vapour. Sometimes, issues related to other members can be discussed, but to find solutions. On the opposite, it translates into an epidemic.

In Proverbs 10:18, the Bible says, 'He that hideth hatred with lying lips, and he that uttereth a slander, is a fool'. The Scripture refers to you as a fool when you don't understand the ways of the Lord, when you cannot recognise the strategies of Satan and when you carry out activities that glorify Satan. When you engage in slandering, the Bible tags you a fool. So whenever you hear of an incident, please verify its veracity and causes before commenting and think wisely before you speak. Remain careful of how you make deductions. For instance, if you sit with a friend chatting and leave your cell phone on a table to go quickly attend to an issue and on your return, he's gone for whatever reason and at the same time you couldn't find your phone, naturally you would be tempted to believe he stole it, even without investigating. But it's also likely that he left on an emergency and in his absence, somebody else used the opportunity to pick up the phone before your return. If the latter was true, but you believed your friend illegally converted your phone into his and you begin to transmit that information, others would help transmit, leading to the destruction of your friend's character. And let me tell you the trouble. You and those who transmitted that message would be held responsible by our Lord Jesus. Even though they didn't witness the scene, but because they transmitted false information, they would have to answer to the Almighty God.

Reckless speeches can be eternally wrecking. Think about the effect of your words before discharging them. Sometimes, a thief would pray, 'Oh God, don't let them catch me today'. And a man, regarding fornication, would say, 'God would help me capture that girl'. The Almighty God talks about not using His name in vain. It's not just about calling Him at random. But whenever you mention His name to support satanic operations, you are employing His name in vain, and the Almighty God might hold you guilty of blasphemy. Negative confession against yourself and others can also be devastating. Words are powerful. If you have a healthy relationship with our Lord Jesus, your words will be wrapped up in the power of the Holy Spirit. When you speak or write, heaven endorses it. So if you say to someone, 'You would die tomorrow', it might come to pass if not spiritually countered. The chief Dark-angel also monitors your speech and as long as it's not beneficial to heaven, he fights to make it happen.

The Bible says, 'For as he thinketh in his heart, so is he' – Proverbs 23:7. This can be paraphrased as 'As a man speaketh, so is he'. Because if you go to Matthew 12:34, you'll see '...for out of the abundance of the heart, the mouth speaketh'. Your words emanate from your inner man. Generally, you say what you think. That's why people, sometimes, stimulate you to decipher your thoughts and humanly they only figure it out by what you say or do. So people interpret you by your words, even though they might be wrong in some cases. That's why slander can have negative effects even on you, the slanderer, as you can speak words that implicate you. Slander is a contagion. When you continue talking with a slanderer, you easily get infected and slowly you become a slandering specialist.

Slander Misconception

Slander is not just about discussing people, it's about discussing them negatively. It's about talking ill of them. It involves talking lies of them, deliberately trying to fracture their character. You can discuss people concerning issues. You can talk about an incident involving someone. But it only becomes slanderous when you intend to destroy their image. Sometimes, you don't intend to destroy a person's personality. But when you continue discussing people negatively, it becomes a habit. You can say it with the intent of not wanting to destroy a man's personality. But another who listens might interpret you differently. That's why you need to remain careful of how and what you speak. Gossip is not synonymous with slander. Gossip involves talking casually of people and issues. It includes talking of unverified stories. But gossips can be slanderous, even when discussed without the intent of character murdering. Slander can be an addiction.

Effects of Slander

Condemns you
On the day of judgement, standing before our Lord Jesus, every man would account for every idle word he speaks – Matthew 12:36. Some people just make utterances. They just speak without precaution. They speak without pre-examination of their speeches. Mind what you say, guard your words, think wisely before you speak and let your words speak life and not death. By your words, you shall be justified and by your words, you shall be condemned – Matthew 12:37. As I mentioned earlier, only two personalities have the power to condemn you. That's you and our Lord Jesus. Your own words can condemn your personality. Your own words can destroy your destiny.

Negative Image
Normally, people cannot read your mind, so they judge you by your words. Your words can tag you negatively. It can offer others contradictory views about your real personality. Words unleashed cannot be withdrawn. You can apologize, but the words stay. Your slander can also tag others negatively. This can have a devastating cascaded effect on humanity, including you the slanderer. When Satan identifies a man with a huge assignment, he fights to block it. When he couldn't capture the man's will to manipulate him, he tries to manipulate others to obstruct his assignment. One of the strategies he employs is slandering. He can cause others to stigmatise him. He could bring up a false situation and the servant of God may appear satanic in the eyes of the slanderer. And since slander is a contagion, it spreads to others. This will have a repulsive effect on the servant of God, but the major loss would be to the congregation and the rest of humanity, as

they will be deprived of his assignment. Every man's assignment is unique. True prophets preach the same gospel, but in different forms and with different skills. They preach the gospel, but with different gifts. Two preachers can teach on the same subject, one you can thoroughly understand and the other you might not.

Slander can get you into trouble

Your words can be slanderous, even to you. Your words can get you into trouble. There are some statements you make about people or issues that implicate you. They might seem normal to you. But to others, they appear slanderous. In the court or judiciary, words are very important. Legal personalities care about validity and invalidity. They're not much bothered about truth or falsity. They only consider a situation as true or false, when it's valid and proven to be true or false. You might be true. You might be innocent, but your very words can convict you.

Destroys your Destiny

Your own words can destroy your destiny. A man who guards his mouth guards his destiny. A man who guides his speech guides his life. Some utterances you make can humanly lead you to a path that blocks your destiny and hence, destroy it. In that regard, you wouldn't fulfil your pre-ordained assignment.

Slander can be Catastrophic

Slander can lead to conflict and escalates to catastrophe. When people decide to carry out a deadly mission, it begins with one man. It begins with a sin of the mind and transforms into action through one man. Words can be destructive. You can be slanderous, not just in spoken words, but even in writing. Slander can lead to major conflicts. The

Hutu-Tutsi genocide started with the thought of one man and the power of words accelerated its crystallisation. Slander can lead to an uprise.

Generational Stigmatization

There are some negative statements you make about people that become generational tags. It becomes stigmatization, even to generations yet unborn. In some cases, it might be true. But if you do it with the object of destroying his character, you're guilty of slander. Whenever you say a word against someone, think about its effect on him.

Dealing with Slandering

Slander can be impeded or eliminated by the following:

Acknowledge Slander as Sin
Understand the word of God. Many are not aware that slandering is a sin. Like any other sin, slander can walk you into the kingdom of darkness. When you recognise and accept that slander is a sin and can lead to eternal devastation like any other sin, you would remain careful of how you talk. Whenever you do anything that violates the principles of Christianity, you're obeying Satan. That's why you need to continually read and understand the Bible. Always ask the Holy Spirit to help you understand.

Do not give people things to say
No matter what you do, people will talk. But when you lead a healthy Christian life, they might talk less. However, if they talk, let it not be driven by your own defect. Many people desire applause more than critique. Truly, applause is inspiring. But sometimes, applause serves as a hidden demotivator. You may believe you've arrived and begin to crawl down. Critique can be a demotivator, but critique serves as a healthy platform as well. You can develop more zest and start walking upwards.

So, to the wise, applause is a motivator, but to the foolish, it's a demotivator. And critique is a healthy platform for the wise. But to the foolish, it's unhealthy. So, whether you're criticized or applauded, use it to advance your assignment.

Stop being talkative
When you talk too much, the probability of you becoming a slanderer increases. Think more than you speak. Spend that slandering time thinking or doing something productive. Utilize your time beneficially and stop talking much. Engage yourself in personal developmental projects that capture your time.

Let your discourse remain Christian
Learn to keep your discussions Christian. When you talk, people must see the difference. They must recognise you as a regenerated personality. Christian conversation doesn't mean you just talk about Jesus. You can discuss job issues. You can discuss private projects. You can discuss schooling. But any utterance that violates Christian principles must be bypassed.

Do not wish evil for Others
When you wish good for others, you don't discuss them negatively. When you desire true success for others, you don't try to destroy their personality through abhorrent speeches. Love others, as you love yourself.

Pray
Slander is a contagion. When you speak slanderously, others capture it. They spread it. And if false, you bear the greatest responsibility. But they also share the trouble. If they depart this world with it, they face eternal consequences. Some wouldn't even know they've contravened the commands of our Lord Jesus. Just one slander can get many into the dark kingdom. As I said, being garrulous can be human, but slandering is satanic. Satan uses it to capture your will. So you have to pray against the spirit of slander. It's satanic! It can be eternally destructive!

Chapter XIII

The Reality of Hell

Children who defy their parents in truth have prices to pay. Similarly, when you work against God's word, you see the other side of Jesus. Satan understands the Trinity – He knows our heavenly Father, he believes Jesus is the Son of God, he knows Jesus is God, he comprehends Jesus died and resurrected, he understands the working of the Holy Spirit, but Satan still lives in rebellion. Satan knows there is heaven. He knows there is hell. He has great knowledge of what the bible teaches. Matthew 4:6 says, 'And saith unto Him, if thou be the son of God, cast thyself down: for it is written, He shall give His angels charge concerning thee: and in their hands they shall bear thee up, lest at any time, thou dash thy foot against a stone'. That was Satan struggling to acquire obeisance from our Messiah. He says, 'It is written', and it is written. If you go to Psalms 91: 11-12, you will see 'For He shall give His angels charge over thee, to keep thee in all thy ways. They shall bear thee up in their hands, lest thou dash thy foot against a stone'. So if you believe Satan doesn't understand scriptures, then you will receive a surprising package with an overflow of spiritual disappointment. In Luke 4:34, a man with an unclean spirit cried, '...let us alone: what have we to do with thee, thou Jesus of Nazareth? Art thou come to destroy us? I know thee who thou art; the Holy One of God'. That was a dark angel speaking through that man when Jesus made an advance to set him free from the trap of Satan. The dark angels know Jesus. So if you trust in the holy doctrine and still walk in demonic disobedience, then how different are you from Satan and his agents?

Hell is real! Many people, even some Christians, do not want to hear you talk about the reality of hell. But it does exist and you must understand its spiritual purpose. There is a misleading myth that hell is owned by Satan. Some believe hell was set up by Satan. But undoubtedly, hell is not owned by Satan. It wasn't set up by Satan. Hell was established by the Almighty God to torture Satan and his dark angels, but man can choose to spend eternity with them. You can decide to live with Satan and his fallen angels infinitely. If you decide to remain an enemy of the Almighty God, your choice to spend eternity with Satan will be approved. Some people murmur that Jesus is not wicked to throw man into hell. Yes, Jesus is not wicked. Assuming the constitution of Sierra Leone enshrines that anybody found guilty of robbery must be sentenced to ten years imprisonment. If you're convicted of robbery and sentenced to ten years in jail, would you tag the judge wicked? Jesus is not wicked. He's just exhibiting his disciplinary characteristic. When Satan rebelled against the Almighty in heaven, He kicked him out, followed by his supporters – the dark angels. When traders misused the house of God into a market place, Jesus overturned their businesses and ejected them. Is that callousness? No, Jesus was angry for righteousness. He was furious because the people wanted to make His father's house a place of commerce. Jesus gets angry with everyone who decides to join Satan in his rebellion. So throwing man into hell is not even an atom of wickedness, but a penalty for violating the heavenly constitution. Jesus loves man so much. He doesn't want man to spend eternity in hell. That's why He designed the holy Bible to guide us and supported that by sending the Holy Spirit – to help us understand His word and to empower us against Satan. Jesus is personally revealing Himself to man as well, all in the fight to save humanity from eternal torture. But that help is truly subject to your will. You can choose to accept it or you can decide to reject it. Not everyone that proclaims the name of our Lord Jesus will enter the kingdom of heaven, except those that do the will of the Almighty God - Matthew 7:21. Generally, the will of the Almighty God is to subdue Satan. His will is to destroy the works of darkness. When Jesus was departing the earth, He instructed all men on one assignment – the Great Commission. And He empowered different Christians with different gifts to carry out that assignment. By the different gifting, every Christian carries out his assignment uniquely. But the ultimate goal is soul-winning. In that regard, God's will for you is to carry out your assignment and maintain your salvation. So, if you don't carry out His will, you would be eliminated from the trip to heaven. Remember, there're only two eternal options – heaven and hell.

Heaven

Heaven is the Almighty God's habitat. Heaven is where the throne of the Trinity sits. The Almighty God doesn't live alone in His eternal residence. He lives with a host of angels. He lives with saints. Around His throne are the four beasts and twenty-four elders who worship Him daily. The four beasts and twenty-four elders fall all day and worship the Almighty God in front of His throne, crying, ' Holy, holy, holy is the Lord, for He alone is worthy'. The angels cry, ' Holy is the Lord'. The saints and all inhabitants of heaven worship the Almighty God, without ceasing. In heaven, there is no darkness, for the Lord Himself illuminates the entire domain. There is no disease. There is no sickness. There is no need, as everything is available in excess. The nature and dialect of heaven is love. In heaven, there is no place for bitterness. There is no room for hate. There is no room for grief. There is no room for division. The Scripture says, 'A city divided against itself will never stand'. So heaven is a unified palace, where everyone speaks with one voice. Everyone speaks one language. All occupants speak the language of the Almighty God, which is love. Every being in heaven operates in the will of the Almighty God. There is no racial segregation. There is no ethnic fight. There is no intercontinental conflict. There is no political fight. The streets of heaven are made of precious substances more precious than the precious elements on the surface of the earth. Nothing dies in heaven. Even the trees do not wither. Heaven is perfect but humanity is imperfect. So the Almighty God transforms humanity into a perfect personality to fit into His perfect domain. That's why the Holy Spirit is here – to walk us into the perfection of Jesus Christ. The Almighty God loves music. So the hosts of heaven play instruments as they worship Him. As on earth, there is a hierarchy, which starts with the Trinity. You have the Father. You have the Son and then the Holy Spirit. You have the four beasts and twenty-four elders who surround and bow before His throne always, to worship Him. There is the archangel Michael. There's angel Gabriel and a host of other angels who take instructions from Michael and Gabriel. All activities of heaven are controlled by the Trinity. The Trinity is a Triune being, functioning as a unified personality. So heaven waits to receive of the Almighty God's creation who would prove themselves worthy to enter into the Holy of Holies. And even among the saints, humans who make it to heaven, there is a hierarchy. The Bible talks of crowns according to how you execute your assignment on earth. But whether you receive a crown or not, strive to enter. Heaven is a permanent place. When you make it there, you live happily forever and ever. Missing heaven would be an eternal regret.

Hell

Hell is the place designed for Satan and his agents. Everything the Almighty God does, He does it perfectly. When He designed heaven for His dwelling and to accommodate beings loyal to Him, He designed it perfectly. And when He designed hell to accommodate His disobedient creatures, He designed it perfectly, as well. Hell was not designed for man! But when you choose to obey Satan, when the chief dark angel remains your master, hell would be your eternal home. Hell is a place of everlasting torture. The Almighty God is the Creator of the universe. He is the Author of every existing and non-existing entity. Even Satan and Lucifer was created by the Almighty God. But by sinful nature, Satan is wicked. So God allows him and his demons to deal with disobedient children. But in the end, even Satan, together with his dark angels, will be dumped into hell. As there is a hierarchy in heaven, there are different positions in hell. There are different places in hell, for different levels of torture. There is the lake of fire, which burns with brimstone. There is the outer darkness. There is the bottomless pit. All these are different designations for different domains of eternal persecution. Other sections of hell are reserved for other disobedient beings. But the bottomless pit is reserved for Satan when his time is up. Hell is a place of everlasting torture. It's a place of eternal torment. Like heaven, if you're judged to hell, you live there forever and ever. There is nothing good in hell. Hell is full of total darkness. There is continuous wailing and gnashing of teeth, as the torture is unbearable.

In Matthew 10:28, Jesus says, 'And fear not them which kill the body, but are not able to kill the soul: but rather fear him which is able to destroy both soul and body in hell'. Satan and his agents can do all in their limited capacity to destroy you. But they can only destroy the mortal side of you – the body. They cannot touch the soul. Only our Lord Jesus has the power to destroy your immortality. Jesus loves man so much but hates sinful actions. He loves the sinner, but He hates the sin. When you continue in sin, He dissociates from you, because He cannot play with immorality. That's why when Jesus touches a man, his iniquity translates into purity. When a man touches Jesus his condemnation transforms into commendation. But when a man chooses to remain in satanic disobedience, his earthly presence will represent a futile existence. In that case, when Jesus looks at you, all He sees is contamination. And when you depart this world devoid of repentance, He has no other option, but to help you live with your friends in hell, because He cannot live with impurity. So, as a rebellious entity, Jesus throws you into hell, not because He hates you, but because you're wrapped up in iniquity. He would want to live with you, but He cannot live with immorality. He would want to dine with you, but He cannot dine with iniquity. His word is His word. In Matthew 13:40-42, Jesus says, 'As therefore the tares are gathered and burned in the fire; so shall it be in the end of the world. The son of man shall send forth His angels, and they shall gather out of His kingdom all things that offend, and them which do iniquity; And shall cast them into a furnace of fire: there shall be wailing and gnashing of teeth'. At the end of time, Jesus would separate the children of God from the children of Satan. Then, the satanic offspring will be thrown into the domain of darkness.

As end-time unfolds, Christians must modify that chocolate gospel. You must let humanity see the real side of the heavenly gospel. It might be difficult, but man must truly understand the implications of obedience and disobedience to the word of the Almighty God. During a trip, travelling from the mine to Freetown, something dropped into my spirit. The Almighty God wants you to know that the gospel of our Lord Jesus is the gospel of judgement, enveloped in love. He provides humanity His word, through the holy Scriptures – the Bible. His word is love, but it's that same word that would be used to judge you. This is not to scare you, but to help you understand the ramifications of obeying Satan, and to guide you into a holy trajectory. Our Lord Jesus revealed a model of His word. It's like a chicken egg, heated at a temperature to an edible state. The shell represents the part man cannot eat. It's the hardest substance of the egg that represents the part of the gospel Christians cannot handle. So, Jesus, Himself had to eat the shell. That is the 'sacrifice' He made for us. That's His death. He died because we cannot pay that price, so He had to do it for us. The egg white represents the area of 'Love' of the gospel. The egg yolk represents the 'Judgemental' part of the gospel. When Jesus removed the shell, He presents the egg to humanity. People, who immediately and permanently reject the egg, face judgement and are catapulted straight to hell. When you receive the egg, Jesus advises you to eat the egg white and not the yolk. He admonishes you to work in love, to obey His voice, to accept the statutes of heaven. But as you eat the egg white, you realize it's so easy to get into the egg yolk. Some people unintentionally get into the yolk, as they eat the white. But when they realize, they step out again. And as long as they have the egg, they get forgiven by the Almighty God. But others eat the white and eat the yolk, with no realization. Even when some realize it, they couldn't get out because they're bound. And until they're delivered, they face judgement. So, the gospel of Jesus is presented in love. But when you reject that charity, when you violate its principles, you see the other side of Jesus. Sin appears rosy to man. It looks sweet, it seems beneficial, but the consequences are devastating. From medical sciences, the cholesterol content of an egg is truly resident in the yolk. Like sin, the egg yolk seems delicious; you enjoy eating it, but its end product can be detrimental. The negative effect of the abnormal presence of cholesterol in the human circulatory system is subtle. It gradually builds up wax-like substances on the inner walls of your blood vessels. It clogs the vessel. And when it matures, the blood vessel becomes blocked by that plaque. If the coronary artery flow, for instance, is interrupted, the heart becomes deficient of blood and oxygen, which leads to a heart attack, and might result in cardiac arrest, and hence death. If the brain is deprived of sufficient blood flow and oxygen, it leads to stroke, which might cause abnormal functioning of any part of the body related to the affected blood vessel pathway. For example, it causes paralysis, reduced or loss of memory and reasoning strength, and even death. This is how sin destroys humanity. The human body itself generates the required cholesterol chiefly through the liver, so ingesting an excess of it with abnormal value causes you more trouble – although its production can be regulated. Also, without physical contact, sin can be internally generated through the mind, which can also be controlled. So, engaging in physical sinful acts leads to more spiritual disaster.

Sometimes, you think you are the best when you are involved in sin. Other times, you're tempted to think you own the world until its effect becomes evident. The result of sin is not only temporary, but eternal as well. It destroys your body, deforms your soul and depletes your spirit. In many cases, you only realize it when it's too late. Our Lord Jesus loves mankind. But when you continually reject His word, you renew His wounds. You remind Him of His persecution. And consequently, you become part of Satan's rebellious army and God sees you as an enemy. Do you know what it takes to become an enemy of God? The Almighty God is loving. But remember, He is also judgemental. Eat the 'egg white' and not the 'egg yolk'. But if you decide to do otherwise, you'll see the other side of Jesus. To carry out his devilish plan, Satan establishes an army.

The Army of Satan

Unknown to many, Satan is busy enlisting combatants into his army. In the normal state, no human is wiser than Satan. It's only God who is more intelligent than the devil. So if you refuse to submit to the Almighty God, then your will can be easily subdued by Satan. Satan hypnotizes you as he desires. The Bible says, '...greater is He that is in you than he that is in the world' – 1 John 4:4. Any man without the Holy Spirit, including Satan, is included in the world. So, you only become wiser than Satan when the Holy Spirit resides in you. Whether you agree or not, if you refuse to get into God's Army, then you will be recruited into the army of Satan. You must acknowledge that in an army, all members are soldiers, but not all physically engage in fighting like the infantry. Some might be in the administrative section. You might not be directly involved in practices like those of the underworld or witchcraft. But you may still be in the army of Satan because you bring honour to his name, by disobeying our Lord Jesus Christ. Remember, sin is obedience to Satan or disobedience to God. That is Satan's plan, for man to defy God. Satan has warriors who are demons – the dark angels that operate mostly in human forms. To make their assignments easier, they rush into humans for accommodation. And the demonic humans begin to behave like the dark angels. Generally, Satan despises activities related to heaven. But he cannot fight against Jehovah. He has no power to directly wage war against Jesus. So Satan fights against the tangibility of God's creativity. He fights to destroy God's creation. The Almighty God loves us so much and gets exasperated whenever Satan touches one of us –Satan knows that! Revelation 12:12 says, 'Therefore rejoice, ye heavens, and ye that dwell in them. Woe to the inhabitants of the earth and of the sea! For the devil is come down unto you, having great wrath, because he knoweth that he hath but a short time'. The earth is in trouble because the chief dark angel is fighting with great vexation to win mankind in the limited time he has. Satan aims to throw as many humans as he can into hell because he doesn't desire to see God's creation live with Him in heaven. He wants humanity to suffer with him in hell, in the end. But Jesus deeply loves us, so when Satan fights against His creation, He sees it as struggling to pull down the reality of His formation.

During universal Christian events like 25th December on which we celebrate the birth of Jesus Christ, demons intensify their attacks on Christians and increase their level of deception to reinforce the unbelief of non-Christians. They stimulate Christians to be distracted from their assignments. Satan arouses Believers to engage in so many secular activities and gets them fatigued to handle spiritual matters. When they get home, they couldn't pray, they couldn't read the word of God, let alone fast and they become spiritually powerless. This does not only affect Christians but makes soul-winning activities more difficult. No wonder Christmas is being widely celebrated in immorality, rather than holiness. You're celebrating the birth of the holy Son of God, then why don't you celebrate Him in purity? Why don't you celebrate Jesus in consecration? Many people can't celebrate Jesus in holiness because, unknowingly, their will has been subjugated by Satan. In some cases, Satan ensnares Christians in sin, which leads to backsliding. In other cases, the devil attacks stubborn Christians with diseases, road, sea and air accidents, and even obstructs their financial flow, to stop them from executing the Great Commission. Physically, the dark angels attack Christians in different forms. Sometimes, they use Unbelievers to help walk Christians out of their God-given tasks. He can get them into sins like sexual immorality and burglary. Some Christians argue that Jesus was not born on 25th December. But whether Jesus was born on 25th December or not, the fact is that 25th December has been set aside to globally celebrate the birth of our Messiah. You can be born on 20th January and choose to celebrate your birth on 30th January. So the issue should not be with the date, but with how you celebrate the birth of our Saviour. Remember, you're not celebrating the date – you're celebrating the birth of Jesus Christ. So as Christmas approaches, the commander-in-chief of the devilish army, Satan, introduces hidden strategies to help his commanders enlist trainees. The Bible says in 1Peter 5:8, 'Be sober, be vigilant; because your adversary the devil, as a roaring lion, walketh about, seeking whom he may devour'. You can see that Satan aims to destroy humanity. But he cannot do it without your will. And only gains control of your will when you breach God's instructions – when you refuse to submit to Jesus. Satan only controls you when you obey him. So, remain sober, do not yield to the devil, recognise satanic strategies and always remember Satan is desperately seeking human recruits to enlist into his army.

Fight to evade everlasting torment and always remember, hell is real!

Chapter XIV

The End-time Army

Jesus is fortifying the End-time army to help restore the lost holy characteristics of the existing church. The primary purpose of the End-time army is to prepare Christians for the second coming of our Lord Jesus Christ. As Jesus does this, He empowers heavenly human soldiers with special gifts, as they break through strongholds of Satan. Christians are losing and so Jesus is implementing another, believed to be His final strategy, to take back the world from Satan. The End-time army is a special task force in the Church, with a specific assignment to make Christians ready to welcome our Lord Jesus when He returns for His bride. As they carry out their assignment, Jesus empowers Christians with diverse spiritual gifts and different talents to attack Satan on every side. The End-time army focuses on holiness, empowered by the Holy Spirit, without which no man shall see God. Yes, the Almighty God cares about our total wellbeing, as it helps us carry out our various tasks. But, the End-time army is designed to nurture Christians to a point of realization that they can handle spiritual fights, as they yield to our Lord Jesus. Many times, Christians wonder why Christians struggle in soul-winning. But if you take a deep look back, you would figure out that the Church is truly divided. Christians always believe they understand the scriptures more than anyone else. But there's a scripture Christians always reveal to Unbelievers, forgetting they're also entangled in it. If you keep warning Unbelievers and baby Christians about issues you're guilty of, then how do you expect to succeed in the Christian race? How would you triumph in the heavenly journey? Christians always recite, '…house divided against itself shall not stand' – Matthew 12:25. This is a very familiar quote among Christians. During a worship session, in a service, some time ago, I got slain in the spirit for more than thirty minutes, on the final day of an eight-day fasting and prayer command from the Lord. The anointing was so strong and the Lord Jesus was certainly investigating my activities. At that time, I was deep into the world. I was deep into immorality, especially sexual. The Lord was asking me about what I gained from the worldly activities I was engaged in. One of the questions I remembered was, 'What do you gain from fornication?' Fornication was my major weakness and I couldn't answer. I was just weeping and asking for mercy, with a desire to make a turnaround. And afterwards, our Lord Jesus gave me a message for the church, which I wrote on a piece of paper and submitted to the media team, as I had no chance to say it orally. Another reason I didn't reveal some of my encounters with Jesus is that I knew I had a writing assignment. And many of the messages I receive from God, I write and reserve for future publications. But the Holy Spirit is making me aware that I must fight to reveal them as soon as possible because many souls are waiting to receive those messages. He says some have already departed, some are dying and some will be deceased without hearing those messages. That's why He is now asking me to use every medium I gain access to, in helping bring back lost souls into His kingdom. He wants me to use every writing opportunity to help win souls and to guard Christians, especially leaders. In an excerpt of the message to the body of Christ, the Lord Jesus says, 'The contemporary church is divided'. And He continued, 'A house divided against itself would never stand'. He says Christians would only succeed when they are united, and they would only be united when they walk in love. He says the Church do not walk in love because they do not allow the Holy Spirit to rule. He says if the Church allows the Holy Spirit to rule, Unbelievers would run into the church, which would make soul-winning much easier. He continued, 'But you struggle in soul-winning because you do not allow the Holy Spirit to rule. How then, can you succeed in evangelism?' How can we fight and defeat the powers of darkness when we are divided? We must take a look back to purify and unite the Christian body, and then we would be ready to confront and conquer the army of Satan. Jesus says if a man has a hundred sheep and loses one, He would run after the lost one and celebrate when he finds it – Matthew 18:12-13. But I tell you now, that when the man is going after the lost one, if he realizes the ninety-nine are negatively scattered, he would run back to protect them. What Jesus was emphasizing is that every soul is important to Him. It doesn't mean the ninety-nine are insignificant. But He's not bothered about them because they're fine. It's like a father who has three children. Two are well-behaved, but the third causes him trouble – the one who gets him to run out of the house and to the police to rescue him. He would not be bothered about the two, who possess moral values, but would always be upset and run to save the troublesome child. This same principle applies to the kingdom of the Almighty God. Our God is not worried about those who're already born again. He's not bothered about those who're saved. He's not troubled about His obedient children. He's worried about lost souls – the disobedient children. So, as ministers of the gospel of our Lord Jesus, you go after Unbelievers to get them into the kingdom of God, forgetting you are losing the won-souls. You believe it's only Unbelievers that are lost, but if you investigate the Church, you would uncover you're continually losing souls you once won. A backslidden Believer is considered an Unbeliever. So, what you need to do now, as you go after Unbelievers, you need to take a look back to ensure the won-souls remain won. You need to ensure the ninety-nine sheep are intact. Our Lord Jesus is raising the end-time army to clean up the Church, to secure Christians, to protect the won-souls, to genuinely convert Unbelievers, to expose and destroy the works of Satan. As you carry out the Great Commission, as you evangelise, take a look back to ensure your congregation is safe. Remember, humanity is already living in the end-time. Let's now see how the end-time army is empowered to succeed in the ministry.

The End-time Army and the Gifts of the Holy Spirit

Like talents, the Almighty God distributes different spiritual gifts to different Christians to help them succeed against Satan. These spiritual gifts work with talents to enable Christians to carry out their various assignments. There are many spiritual gifts, but I'll discuss the nine major gifts, as stated in 1 Corinthians 12: 8 – 10. These spiritual gifts include the Word of Wisdom, Word of Knowledge, Faith, Healing, Miracles, Prophecy, Discernment, Tongues and Interpretation of Tongues. But these nine spiritual gifts are offspring of the Holy Spirit. And so, to receive any of those gifts, you firstly need to have an indwelling of the Holy Spirit. This comes after you get born again. The Holy Spirit comes instantaneously after the baptism of the Holy Spirit, mostly through a servant of God. And in many cases, the Holy Spirit makes the spiritual deposit on arrival. He comes simultaneously with the gift. Briefly, we would discuss these gifts. Generally, there are nine gifts of the Holy Spirit, which our Lord Jesus uses to equip the church. He uses them to help Christians carry out their assignment by destroying the works of Satan and help bring back lost souls into the kingdom of the Almighty God. But the Almighty God empowers the end-time army specifically with those gifts, some of which I will categorize under the following subheadings:

Word of Wisdom

Wisdom is very essential in ministry. Christians need to be able to apply the word of God appropriately in different situations to help others. They need to be able to apply Christian principles to settle Christian disputes and conflicts relating to Unbelievers as well. Christians need to be able to apply the word of God in specific situations in soul-winning. Christians need to be able to bring solutions to earthly problems through this wisdom that comes from the Almighty God. Solomon asked God for wisdom to rule his people and the Almighty God made him the wisest king/man on earth, in his time. So, God offers some Christians this gift to help others. You can be full of knowledge, but if you lack divine methodologies from God, your knowledge may remain meaningless.

Word of Knowledge

Knowledge is important. Christians should know the God they serve. They should know and understand the principles of heaven. They should know the word of God. Some Christians are so gifted in memorizing and understanding scriptures. Whatever they discuss, they know which scriptures to use and where to find them instantly. They don't struggle to find scriptures – It's just part of them. But a major benefit of this gift is similar to the gift of revelation, in which God reveals information your human senses couldn't capture. For instance, if somebody steals your pen, the Holy Spirit can reveal it to you through this gift. So God offers Christians this gift to function well in the ministry.

Faith

Faith is about believing in the unseen. It's about hoping without evidence. So, in faith, you have to believe and hope without proof. The Scripture says that without faith, it's impossible to please God. You worship God, even when you don't see Him. You talk to Him and are not even sure if he hears you, but you just believe He hears and will respond. When you desire something, you just pray and believe it will happen. Every Christian should have faith, but genuinely many Christians waver sometimes. The principle of faith is universal, but God offers some the gift of faith who do not doubt at all in anything they do. As long as they're convinced, they just do it and believe it will happen and God supports their trusting in Him.

Healing

Healing is also a fundamental need in the ministry. When Christians get sick, they find it difficult to carry out their assignments. And sometimes they can't work at all. The Almighty God offers some Christians the gift of healing to help others, especially in illnesses doctors could not handle. You can be full of knowledge and wisdom, but if you don't have the physical strength, your spiritual desire to save souls will remain an imagination. The Almighty God heals supernaturally, but Christians have a responsibility to keep themselves in good health, by adhering to personal hygiene and abstaining from activities that are disease friendly.

Miracles

When Jesus started His ministry on earth, He did a miracle at a wedding party, when He turned water into wine. Miracles are not only for Christians, they exist to help Unbelievers as well. It also helps to demonstrate the power of the Almighty God, which can draw Unbelievers to our Lord Jesus. So God offers some Christians the gift to do miracles. God gives man the ability to handle earthly affairs, but there're situations humanity cannot control. God uses those occurrences to deliver man and glorify Himself.

Prophecy

The gift of prophecy is one of the important, if not the most important, gifts in ministry. Mostly, the Almighty God transmits messages to His people directly through this gift. Other times, He does it indirectly. God can reveal the past, present and future occurrences to His children. So He offers some Christians this gift.

Discernment

When you encounter satanic agents, you're supposed to be able to recognise them. When a Christian steps into a demonic environment, he should be able to know. By this gift, Christians can recognise phoney prophets and their associates. So our Lord Jesus offers some Christians the gift of discernment to recognise satanic implementation. This helps in pulling down the strongholds of Satan.

Tongues

Lack of understanding of the gift of tongues is causing scriptural division in the Church. Many do not believe in this gift. Some say it only existed in the days of the Apostles of Jesus Christ. Others argue that it has to be a known language. The Almighty God uses this gift as well, to convey messages to His people. Tongues can be known languages and it can also be unknown languages. In Acts 1:8, when the disciples of Jesus were in the upper room praying, on the day of Pentecost, a mighty wind rushed in, overwhelmed the people and Unbelievers who came around heard them speak in their languages. That was a demonstration of the power of God through a known tongue. If you go to 1Corinthians 14:2, you would realize that 'whosoever speaketh in an unknown tongue speaketh mysteries. He speaketh not unto men, but unto God, for no man understandeth him'. In this sense, it's a language unknown to men. It's a heavenly language. So God offers some Christians this gift for spiritual communications. Be careful, as there are satanic tongues as well. The chief dark angel duplicates heavenly practices and the tongue is no exception. But that's why the spirit of discernment exists.

Interpretation of Tongues

Tongues, whether known or unknown, without interpretation, are of no benefit to the Church. That's why Jesus says you should pray for interpretation −1 Corinthians 14:13. Tongues are messages from the Almighty God. They are meant to edify the Church and draw Unbelievers towards our Lord Jesus. So the Almighty God offers some Christians this gift to interpret His encoded messages. When I just got saved, I operated on this gift. Most times it comes as unknown, but the interpretation comes mostly through me and sometimes through others. At a particular time, my tongue sounded like Chinese, whilst I was alone in my bedroom, worshipping the Almighty God.

I believe you now have an understanding of what those gifts mean. There are other spiritual gifts like the Gift of Mercy, which is a gift exhibited by Christians who forgive easily. You hurt them and the next minute you're forgiven – they don't hold grudges, they don't hate. They don't accommodate resentment. The Almighty God distributes the different gifts of the spirit to different Christians. For the end-time army to succeed, all Christians operating in the different gifts must work as a team. But to get a deeper understanding of how these gifts are employed in the ministry, we need to examine the concept of combinational gifts.

Combinational Gifts

The different gifts of the spirit are separate gifts that are offered separately to different Christians. But in practice, multiple gifts are employed in many cases. The Scripture says, 'If you have faith as a mustard seed, you shall say to this mountain be thou removed and be cast into the sea and it shall be done'. This refers to faith applied by Christians in deplorable situations they are faced with – situations that seem humanly impossible. That scripture reveals that as long as your faith is strong, you would move mountains. In other words, you would speak to dying situations and they would resuscitate. You would command demons and they would obey. But faith is a gift of the Spirit, which implies there are specific Christians with the gift of faith. These are Christians who operate in the ministry without a grain of doubt. They speak to situations and believe it would happen without wavering. This teaches us that to do extraordinary miracles, you need the gift of faith. So we see that both the Gift of Faith and the Gift of Miracles can operate simultaneously from one man. However, some do not emit miracles, but whenever they're faced with situations they just believe it would be fine. Also, to operate in the Gift of Healing, you need the Gift of Faith. In a real sense, the Gift of Healing is a subset of the Gift of Miracles. Divine healing is a miracle and so they work together. Others work by merging and at this point, you should be able to make that deduction. Now that we have understood the concept of combinational gifts, we would now move on to how these gifts of the spirit are used in ministry. There are different offices in Christian ministries that employ these spiritual gifts. They include five major offices. These are the offices of the Apostle, Prophet, Evangelist, Pastor and Teacher. Let's now take a brief look at them, concerning the gifts of the spirit.

The Office of the Apostle

During the days when our Lord Jesus physically existed on earth, He commissioned His disciples as Apostles, with Paul as the least, after Jesus was betrayed by Judas. Those Apostles were ordained by our Lord Jesus. Today, there are servants of God who claim to operate in the office of the Apostle. I couldn't tell how they're ordained. But they might be right if they truly have a relationship with our Lord Jesus. If you take a look at Paul's situation, you would get an evidential clue. Paul was not among the twelve disciples, commissioned as Apostles by our Lord Jesus. He did not work with Jesus when He existed on earth. Paul, also known as Saul, only had a spiritual encounter with our Lord Jesus, after His resurrection, which directed his path into the office of the Apostle, after being ordained by the other Apostles. Apostles are very powerful in ministry. They hold the highest office in Christian ministries. Generally, Apostles operate with multiple spiritual gifts. They have the gift of wisdom and knowledge. They have faith. They do miracles. They can prophesy.

The Office of the Prophet

In our time, the prophetic office is one of the most, if not the most, powerful office. Prophets also operate in multiple spiritual gifts. For instance, when they prophesy, if their prophecy is about satanic oppression against a Christian, they can fix the situation by the power of the Holy Spirit and in the name of our Lord Jesus. This means they prophesy and execute miracles. And to do miracles, they must have the gift of faith. Prophets also are generally gifted with the word of wisdom and knowledge. Someone can have the gift of prophecy, but that doesn't make him a prophet.

The Office of the Evangelist

Evangelists are specialized in soul winning. They have ministerial strategies to help bring Unbelievers into the kingdom of the Almighty God. To help win souls, they need to be skillful in preaching the word. So evangelists have the gifts of wisdom and knowledge. And to draw Unbelievers closer, they do miracles. So they have the gift of faith, as well.

The Office of the Pastor

Generally, pastors teach their congregation the word of God. And so, they are mainly gifted with wisdom and knowledge. Local pastors are heads of local churches – a congregation with a pastor as the shepherd. To interpret scriptures appropriately, pastors need the gifts of knowledge and wisdom. Pastors are also gifted in faith, as you can't teach people what you do not believe in. Some pastors might have other spiritual gifts, as desired by our Lord Jesus, like the working of miracles.

The Office of the Teacher

Like pastors, teachers also help Christians understand the word of God. And so, they need the gifts of wisdom and knowledge. To teach, they also need the gift of faith, as they can't teach what they do not trust. Like other Christians, teachers can have other spiritual gifts.

As there are combinational gifts, there are also combinational offices, which we'll now take a snap look at.

Combinational Offices

This refers to Christian offices that are combined. For instance, a teacher can be a pastor and a pastor can also operate in the office of a teacher.

A prophet can be a pastor, etc. To get more understanding of how these gifts operate in ministry, I discuss some of the spiritual gifts and offices to see how they are interrelated.

The Spirit of Discernment

In this end-time, the discerning spirit is a fundamental gift in ministry. The Almighty God empowers Christians to decode demonic activities. Many people are deceived because they cannot make a distinction between what is right and what is not right. They do not know the difference between good and evil. They cannot figure out the activities of Satan. They cannot recognise phoney prophets. Ministry, and all Christians, would hardly succeed without the spirit of discernment. Many people get it wrong – they want to use only the human mind to discern spiritual applications. You cannot use just your human intellect to interpret spiritual occurrences. You employ a spiritual mind to interpret spiritual issues. You would never recognise a satanic agent just by viewing with your human eyes. This is one of the relevance of holiness. This is why purity is significant. Yes, the spirit of discernment is a spiritual gift. But God searches for available vessels to work with – vessels to reveal His activities to, vessels to reveal demonic activities to. Our Lord Jesus knows Satan is stepping up strategies to fight against Christians. So Jesus wants to equip every Christian with discernment. But when you are wrapped up in sin, especially fornication/adultery, you become so insensitive. You could see a dark angel and call it a holy angel. You could see a phoney prophet, and tag him a true prophet. God wants every Christian to be able to discern. Discernment can be a gift, but if you cannot distinguish between a dark angel and a holy angel, then your mental drive would require a spiritual surgery. Demons easily recognise genuine Christians. Satanic agents easily identify God's anointed. Similarly, every Christian is supposed to be able to make a distinction between a satanic follower and a godly agent. I was invited to an anglican service somewhere in northern Sierra Leone. That anglican church had a spiritual system similar to that of the Roman Catholic but diluted with traits of Pentecostalism. They performed candle rituals and did praise and worship sessions as in the charismatic churches. Initially, the bishop offered a few admonitions, accompanied by many candle ceremonials. Afterwards, together with other members of his ministry, he walked around hugging members as a symbol of love and unity. It was an activity in which all members participated. The bishop walked towards our location, embraced me, my colleague-host who was seated by me, and many congregants. He then walked back to his pulpit, as other members assumed their normal sitting positions. After another set of admonitions, the ministry went into a praise and worship session, succeeded by another phase of the love-unity cuddling. Again, the bishop walked towards our seat, got a handshake with my colleague-host and bypassed my warm reception. He walked past me and continued the handshake, as he moved to the back of the religious hall. I thought his action was unintentional, so I intercepted him on his return and stretched forth my right hand to delete the accusation of his first evasion from my memory, but the only thing I could grab was the warm layer of air, which surrounded my expanded palm. He couldn't look at me in the eye. From his face, I could sense a form of internal unrest, which could easily be crushed by an opposing anointing. He avoided making contact with any part of my physical being. And disappointedly, I walked back to my seat, as I stared at his speedy steps towards the glassy lectern. For the rest of the sermon, his evasive action formed the major part of my literal absorption, as thoughts of the supposed spiritual rejection continually repelled utterances from the pulpit. Why his action? I couldn't figure it out. As he was wrapping up, he announced an altar call for long-timers and first-timers. I glanced at my colleague-host, whose eyes emitted a signal of agreement. Approximately six of us left for the altar and as we walked, the bishop projected his fingers in a direction that shifted my prolonged absent-mindedness. Thoughts of his perceived spiritual refusal intensified, as I struggled to restore my evaporating cognizance. I responded, 'Me, sir?' And he nodded with a question, 'Are you a preacher?' Well, being a preacher is sometimes considered a speciality in Christianity, but I never categorised myself in that level. My lips clattered, as I struggled to respond. 'I do Christian articles on Facebook and I tell people about Jesus, that's all'. That was my response and he continued, 'I asked because during the service I saw you in a vision preaching with great anointing'. The bishop further revealed that God wants me to preach to his congregation. I replied, 'If God wants me to do that, He will get me a confirmation'. He smiled and reacted, 'I love that'. When a bishop offers a stranger his pulpit, you know it's deeper than human instrumentation. I knew nothing about him. We've never met before. The bishop never knew me, but the Holy Spirit knew me. The Holy Spirit advertises you when you live for Him. When Jesus made an advance to cast out demons from that demon-possessed man, the demons, through the man, cried, 'Have you come to disturb us before the time, thou holy one of God?' The demons recognised Jesus. They discerned His true personality. The spirit of discernment can be a gift, but every Christian is supposed to be able to distinguish between a dark angel and an angel of the Lord. When you stand in front of a demon, or a satanic agent, he knows if you are a true child of God, which makes it easier for them to attack. They discern your spiritual stature. When you recognise your enemy/opponent, it becomes easier to launch your attack. But when you do not see/know him, you work blindly, which is jeopardising. You can easily get destroyed. That's why our Lord Jesus empowers the end-time army to help them uncover satanic activities. So they'll be able to hit on target and simultaneously guard their spiritual territory. The Holy Spirit reveals, but the spirit of discernment is a special gift, which is a subset of the powers of the Holy Spirit. So, to succeed in ministry, and hence in the Christian journey, you need the spirit of discernment.

The Gift of Revelation

The spirit of discernment is similar, or related to the gift of revelation, in the sense that discernment is also a form of knowing things revealed by the spirit. But the spirit of discernment occurs generally when you face situations. For instance, when you face a phoney prophet, you recognise his true identity. When you get into an environment in which there is a witch, you detect it. But the gift of revelation operates differently. You can be in your home in Sierra Leone, and God reveals information to you about someone living in the United Kingdom. This, most times, happens in dreams and visions. You can be sleeping, whilst God reveals information to you about things to happen ten years later. God speaks to Christians with that gift about things to happen. He shows them future occurrences. You can be in a Christian meeting and see angels moving around. You can see a vision of occurrences in the past. Our Lord Jesus empowers the end-time army with this gift, generally, not only to help themselves but to prepare Christians for present and future occurrences. The Almighty God uses this gift to reveal things of the past, things of the present and things to come.

Prophetic Gift

The prophetic gift is one of the most powerful gifts in Christianity. Prophets have an overflow of the Holy Spirit and an overflow of this gift. Prophets are spokespersons for the Almighty God. This gift is also related to the gift of revelation, as they also decipher things of the spirit. But theirs is at a higher level. The gift of revelation operates at intervals. Sometimes, messages come. Other times, it doesn't come. But with the gift of prophecy, it's a continuous flow. Prophets always see satanic activities. Whenever they face people going through troubles, they see. Whenever they meet with phoney prophets, they recognise them. This happens, even on the spot. It can also happen from a distance. And what makes them more efficient is that they do not only recognise satanic operations, but they are empowered by the Holy Spirit to deal with the situations – they are empowered to fix them. For instance, if a married woman had been barren for five years and it was a witchcraft manipulation, the prophet will see it and deliver the woman by the power of the Holy Spirit and in the name of our Lord Jesus. Many prophets operate with the gift of miracle. But remember, having only the prophetic gift doesn't necessarily make you a prophet.

The Gift of Teaching

Knowing how to teach is a gift. Many Christians and Unbelievers are misled by listening to contradictory doctrines. The Scripture says, ' Faith cometh by hearing and hearing the word of God'. So, whatever you continue hearing develops your faith in the path of that doctrine. The end-time army is more concerned about purity. They're more concerned about your relationship with the Almighty God. Satan can manipulate preachers to infect the Christian doctrine. He deposits demonic impurities into the gospel of our Lord Jesus, through manipulated preachers, to mislead and deceive humanity, especially baby Christians and Unbelievers. And even the very elect might be entrapped. But our Lord Jesus empowers the end-time army with a special gift to unfold the true word of God to His people. Teaching can be done in many ways. Some end-time soldiers carry out teachings of the gospel through verbal preaching. These preachers talk the truth to the congregation. They talk in person or talk through audio recordings. Teaching can also be done through singing. The Almighty God empowers some end-time soldiers to sing. Our heavenly Father created different creatures differently. Some do not like listening to people talking for a long period. They get bored and feel sleepy. But they can listen to songs for hours. They can even lie in bed, listening to songs without blinking. So the Almighty God empowers end-time soldiers to teach His word through music. God loves music! So music is also part of man's divine nature, as we're made in the image and likeness of God. Teaching is also discharged through writing. Writing is a powerful tool in ministry. The holy scriptures that guide us were written by holy servants of the Most High God. Some do not endure verbal preaching for long periods. They don't like listening to songs, but they read materials, they can read books for hours, without taking a step away. So our Lord Jesus empowers His soldiers with the gift of writing. The teaching ministry is also carried in another form, the Movie Ministry, which I would refer to as the Combinational Ministry. The Movie Ministry combines talking, singing and writing –It combines audio and video scenarios. Also, some can get tired of the singular forms of teaching methods, but with the combinational, they hardly get fatigued. They can watch movies for hours, undistracted. And many times, people understand messages better when they see their applications. But to mature spiritually, you need to adapt to all forms of teaching. You might hear a message through talking that you may not hear through singing. In this end-time, without a thorough understanding of the word of God, you can be easily deceived by Satan and his team. When you truly understand the word, you can apply it in your life and cement your relationship with the Lord, and successfully carry out your pre-ordained assignment.

Chapter XV

Get Ready

'And unto the angel of the church in Sardis write; These things saith He that hath The seven Spirits of God, and the seven Stars; I know thy works, that thou hast a name that thou livest, and art dead. Be watchful, and strengthen the things which remain, that are ready to die; for I have not found thy works perfect before God. Remember therefore how thou hast received and heard, and hold fast, and repent. If therefore thou shalt not watch, I will come on thee as a thief, and thou shalt not know what hour I will come upon thee. Thou hast a few names even in Sardis which have not defiled their garments; and they shall walk with me in white: for they are worthy. He that overcometh, the same shall be clothed in white raiment; and I will not blot out his name out of the book of life, but I will confess his name before my Father, and before His angels. He that hath an ear, let him hear what the Spirit saith unto the churches' – Revelation 3:1-6. That's our Lord Jesus, the Alpha and Omega, talking to the Church. Our Lord Jesus always reveals weaknesses and errors of the Church for correction, as His word is His word. These were God's people. But some offended in some ways which our Lord Jesus revealed because He wanted them to repent and be free. He wanted to redeem His people from the traps of Satan. Nevertheless, others remained faithful to the Almighty God and He promises to maintain their names in the book of life. He promises they would live with Him eternally, which He would always do, as His name is Faithful. But the will of the Almighty God is not for a cross-section, or for a few of mankind to remain with Him. His will is for all humanity to remain His children, even after our earthly existence. That's why the Holy Spirit is revealing the strategies of Satan to help save humanity from earthly and eternal devastation. He's revealing Satan's strategies, to walk you into perfection. Our Lord Jesus is employing the music ministry, He's using the writing ministry, and He's using different forms of ministry to protect man from the tricks of Satan, as at the end of time, He's going to judge you, He's going to judge me – He's going to judge the world.

Lucifer, who was a highly anointed heavenly being, rebelled against Jehovah. He attempted to dethrone the Most High – God Forbid, as the Almighty God loved him so much that He brought him closer to Himself. Lucifer, who was the son of the morning, succeeded in convincing approximately a third of the angels of heaven to fight against the Almighty God. But that success in persuading a smaller group of angels of heaven was satanic and led to an eternal failure. Lucifer was kicked out of heaven together with his fallen angels – Revelation 12:7-9. Lucifer then became the arch-enemy of the Almighty God, and hence the chief enemy of man. That's why the scripture says, '…woe to the inhabitants of the earth and of the sea! For the devil is come down unto you, having great wrath, because he knoweth that he hath but a short time' – Revelation 12:12. The earth then became a battlefield for man and Satan. But man was weaker than Satan, as the Almighty God offered man a will independent of His. The Almighty God did not retrieve His power from Satan and his dark angels. He only kicked them out of heaven. However, that power is just a minute fraction of God's power but still superior to man's power. Jehovah knew man was defenceless, so He had to reconcile man onto Himself after the disobedience in the garden of Eden, and empower man by the blood of Jesus and the power of the Holy Spirit. This was accomplished on the Cross of Calvary when Jesus cried 'IT IS FINISHED' – John 19:30. The resurrection of our Messiah empowers Christians when they're washed in His blood and endowed with the Holy Spirit. So Satan cannot manipulate you until he distorts the relationship between you and the Holy Spirit. Satan only captures your will when you submit to his will. But Jesus died and resurrected to help submit your will to the will of the Almighty God. Except on special assignments, Jesus doesn't coerce you to submit your will. It must be your will to submit your will to the will of the Almighty God. Jesus loves you so much, that's why He says, 'Come unto me, all ye that labour and are heavy-laden and I will give you rest'. Jesus wants you to love Him because He first loves you. But He says, 'If ye love me, keep my commandments'. Jesus only proves you love Him when you do what He says, when you obey His words and when you adhere to His instructions. Remember, the same Jesus who says 'Come unto me' is the same Jesus that would say 'Depart from me'. Jesus loves you so much, but when you reject His love, you see the judgemental side of Him.

People normally say 'There's no greater love than a man laying down his life for his fellow men'. Yes, that's what Jesus demonstrated after His ministry on earth, as that was His assignment. But our assignment is not to physically lay down our lives for our fellowmen. Jesus did not instruct us to physically die for our neighbours. He says, 'Love your neighbour'. He says, 'Go ye into the world and preach the gospel to every creature'. The creatures, in this sense, refer to your neighbours – your friends, your family, your other colleagues and even your enemies. So the greatest love man can offer man is to tell man the truth about Jesus – it's to preach our Lord Jesus to your fellow man. Jesus wants you to stay alive for as long as you can, as He wants you to preach the gospel to every man. Our assignment is the Great Commission. Our assignment is soul winning. You must be ready to die for the gospel. But physically laying down your life for your fellowman is not a heavenly assignment and so, it's not a guarantee you would get to heaven. You can be charged for suicide, you can be charged for self-murder when you face our Lord Jesus. So sacrificing your life for your fellow men is not about physically dying for them, but ignoring worldly pleasures and taking up your assignment, in the interest of humanity and heaven.

Do not fear Satan, as the Holy Spirit that's in you is greater than him. At the end of the world, the chief dark angel, that old serpent, the dragon, called Satan, who is the devil will be captured by just one angel from heaven, who would bind and throw him into the bottomless pit for a thousand years and all his deception would be put on hold, as our Lord Jesus reigns with His saints on earth – Revelation 20:1-5. And after the thousand years, Satan would be released for a little while and in the end would be cast into the lake of fire that burns with brimstone where he shall be tormented forever and ever, alongside his demons and agents – Revelation 20:10.

But as you run the Christian race, always remember that generally, man has two major appointments with the Almighty God – death and judgement. The Scripture says '…it is appointed unto men once to die, but after this the judgement' – Hebrews 9:27. Satan has deceived many into believing that everything that happens to man is driven by the Almighty God. They believe anything that befalls them is orchestrated by the Almighty. But that's an outrageous lie from Satan. The Almighty God has a will, man has a will and Satan has a will. The Almighty God and Satan are struggling to gain control of man's will. So your life will be controlled by whom you submit your will to. If you surrender your will to the Almighty God, He controls your affairs. But if you submit your will to Satan, Satan becomes the head of your activities, and Satan's will is to distract, deceive and dehumanise humanity. His goal is to destroy man! That old serpent wants to help throw as many as he can into hell, as he doesn't want to suffer alone in eternity. Satan continues to deceive man in that direction so man would be negligent and make no effort to fulfil The will of the Almighty God. For anything, man would say it is God. But Jesus says, 'If a man loves me, he will keep my words: and my Father will love him, and we will come unto him, and make our abode with him' – John 14:23. When you submit to Jesus, He lives with you – He becomes your friend. And all your activities would be controlled by Him. Jesus wants to embrace you. He wants you to be happy, He wants you to lead a successful life on earth, but only if you would submit to His will.

Many times, when someone departs the earth, some say it's his time. Yes, they're right. But your death-time can be set by the Almighty God, it can be set by you, it can be set by Satan. It can be set by you when you violate the principles of heaven. In Ephesians 6:2-3, the Almighty God says, 'Honour thy father and mother; (which is the first commandment with promise;) That it may be well with thee, and thou mayest live long on the earth'. And in Matthew 15:4, the Almighty God says, 'Honour thy father and mother; and, he that curseth father or mother, let him die the death'. So, if you continually dishonour your parents, you can shorten your lifespan on earth. When Solomon requested wisdom from the Lord, He did not only shower him with wisdom, He gave him riches which he did not even ask for, and promised to lengthen his days if he would walk in His ways to keep His commandments and statutes, as his father David did – 1 Kings 3:11-14. So we see there are biblical conditions that influence your lifespan on earth. Some people perform demonic rituals for whatever reason and they make a covenant with Satan, to send them to eternity on a specific date or send a relation or friend to eternity at a particular time. Satan can set your death-time when you directly work for him as an agent. When you violate his instructions, he can exterminate you, as you have offered him your will. When you work for the Almighty God and He becomes satisfied with your earthly ministry, He can call you home and say, 'Well done thou good and faithful servant' – Matthew 25:21. In other cases, God can destroy you, sending you to eternity when you disobey Him to an extent – Revelation 2:20-22. In Genesis 6:3, the Almighty God says, 'Man shall live for one hundred and twenty years'. That's the will of the Almighty God. He wants us to live for one hundred and twenty years. But at the end of the world, whether you're five years or not, it doesn't matter, as even mothers would be pregnant at that time with unborn babies.

In his ministry, John the Baptist started, 'Repent ye: for the kingdom of heaven is at hand' – Matthew 3:2. When Jesus started His ministry, He cried, 'Repent: for the kingdom of heaven is at hand' – Matthew 4:17. So we see that the gospel of our Lord Jesus is mainly focused on repentance. Man was conceived in sin, delivered in sin. But man has a chance to walk out of sin. You would never have a healthy relationship with our Lord Jesus when you continue in iniquity. And so the only means to let the Almighty God grant you audience to begin the journey to heaven, and remain glued to Him is by repentance. But many, even some Christians, do not truly understand the principles of repentance. They do not understand what repentance is all about. When you hurt God in any way, you confess to Him and ask for forgiveness. But whenever you ask for mercy, it must be followed by a genuine promise. You must commit to God that you would not repeat that act. This is what a lot of people miss. They ask for forgiveness but do not make a promise of not repeating the sin they committed. Your promise tells God you do not intend to redo that act of disobedience anymore. It assures God you regretted that satanic action. But because many desire to continue in sin, they do not make that commitment. For some who genuinely do, whenever you repeat a confessed sin, you're breaking a promise to God. Whenever you confess sins and ask for forgiveness, God looks at your intent. If you desire to continue in that sin, He would know and respond appropriately. So, all your confession would represent a vain supplication. Understand this, man is instructed to forgive as many times as man is hurt. But the Almighty God forgives when He wants to – He can choose to not forgive. We know already, that sin against the Holy Spirit is unforgivable. And we know the Holy Spirit is God. That means there's an extent of sin God doesn't forgive. Whenever you ask for mercy, you hope God forgives. But whether He forgives or not remains His decision. Repentance is not just about confessing and asking for forgiveness. You must understand that repentance is a turnaround. It's swimming out of iniquity you were immersed in. It's an act of total regret, not wanting a recurrence. When man increased in wickedness on earth, God said, '...it repenteth me that I have made them' – Genesis 6:5-7. That means God regretted He made man. In other words, if man's creation could be reversed and He was faced with the thought to make man, He wouldn't do it. This is what repentance is all about. When you ask for forgiveness, you must be in a position not wanting to commit that act again. Remember, the Holy Spirit is always there to help. Friends, hell is not a jesting establishment. Satan keeps fooling man with the temporary pleasures of this world. If you make the wrong decision, you would be wrapped up in everlasting regret. Hell is not a place you reside for a certain period. You stay there forever, in continuous torture. Please make another turn. When the children of Israel caused Moses to sin against God, Numbers 20, the Almighty God emphasized Moses would see the promised land, but would not enter – Numbers 27:12-14. Moses continued to ask for mercy. But he got to a point that the Almighty God got infuriated and instructed Moses to not talk to Him about that matter anymore because His decision on that was final. He emphasized Moses would not enter the land which flowed with milk and honey, and so was it – Deuteronomy 3:23-28. Imagine the relationship Moses had with the Almighty God. So, sometimes, you get so tied up in sin that the principle of repentance couldn't work for you anymore. You would speak to God, but He would remain unresponsive, or firm on a decision against you. Look at how God destroyed some of the children of Israel in the wilderness, when they disobeyed Him. People He considered His own. People He delivered from Egypt. If God can destroy a cross-section of the children of Israel, He can destroy any disobedient child. Hold on to Jesus, and do not cause the Almighty God to make a permanent decision against you.

The Almighty God is merciful. But He offers mercy to whom He desires – Romans 9:15. He presents divine favour to His chosen, and we cannot question that side of Him, but there's something you must understand. In some cases, the Almighty God considers reasons which might be hidden to humanity. If you take a snap look at the life of Saul, you would uncover that if the Almighty God just wanted to stop Saul's persecution of Christians, He had an alternative to instantaneously slay him and that would have been the end of the story. Or He could've allowed Saul to continue his atrocities, but continually subduing him until death and destroy him. But the Almighty God figured out something good in Saul. Yes, Saul was passionate about troubling Christians. He did everything possible in his limited power to preclude Christians from achieving their goal. He fought to repel the gospel of Jesus Christ. That was callous! It was wicked! It was satanic! But the good thing, I believe, the Almighty God saw that Saul was dedicated to his satanic assignment, as he strove tirelessly to pursue his lost vision – wrestling with Christians. So, the Almighty God realized that if He could transform Saul to work for Him, he would make an indelible inscription in the history of Christianity. He realized Saul would become very instrumental in ministry, and that's exactly what he did. We all know what Paul, also called Saul, did after his encounter with Jesus Christ – Acts 26:14-18. We saw how Paul was zealous about saving souls. We all benefit from the contribution of Paul to the holy Scriptures. Paul's transformation also serves as a witness, verifying the true existence of the Almighty God in the sight of gentiles. Even Christians, the disciples, couldn't believe Paul was truly converted, the truth of which attracted more unbelievers to the doctrine of our Lord Jesus. When Abraham concealed the truth about Sarah being his wife, the Almighty God showed him mercy. But why did Abraham not reveal the truth? I am not justifying his action, but I want you to see something in this. Abraham feared not being killed. He knew the people he was dealing with. If he had revealed the truth of Sarah being his wife, he could, or would have been killed. But Abraham did not try to save his life just because he wanted to continue living with his wife, not just because he loved Sarah, not because he wanted to continue in the pleasures of this world. But because he had an assignment he wanted to complete. The Almighty God has the sovereign power to show mercy to whom He chooses. But, sometimes you need to acknowledge the circumstances in which He offers mercy. When He knows you're dedicated to Him. When He knows you're willing to submit to Him. When He acknowledges He can make something good out of you, He can offer unconditional mercy. As a Christian, you know our God is merciful, you know Jesus is loving, but you must strive for excellence, seeing Jesus as our perfect model. The Holy Spirit is here to help us. But generally, when you attempt to sin, the Holy Spirit doesn't slap you in the face to refrain. He advises, and you have the choice to accept or reject. So, as you do ministry, you should have the desire to not disobey the Almighty God in anything and remain committed to living for Him. Our Lord Jesus offers mercy to everyone who acknowledges Him as Lord and Saviour – when you get born again. Jesus deletes your creative sin and erases your sinful past when you bow to Him. But He says, 'I will have mercy on whom I will' – Romans 9:15. This implies God can offer mercy to specific people in specific situations, as He pleases. And the trouble is you're not sure if He would offer you that mercy. When convicts are imprisoned, after a certain period, a president or royal leader can offer what is called a 'prerogative of mercy'. He orders the release of some prisoners who have served a certain period of sentence. But also, the prisoners and even the judiciary would not know the criminals who would be discharged. It comes by surprise, so man should not depend on that. That's why you should not be comfortable in sin. I know there's grace, I know the Almighty God is merciful, I believe in the principle of repentance. I believe in confession and forgiveness of sins, but all I ask is for you to cooperate with the Holy Spirit – to listen to Him, to adhere to His advice, to listen to His directions, to allow His leading and you would lead a healthy Christian life. Offering mercy is the Almighty God's independent decision. The Almighty God is loving, but judgemental, as well. At the end of time, He's going to judge every one of us. That's why He's unravelling the strategies of Satan. And you must note that the judgement of the Almighty God can be generational. When Abraham pleased God, God blessed his seeds, his generations yet unborn. It was Abraham who pleased God, not his seeds. But God blessed his seeds. When Jezebel persecuted God's servants, God says, 'I'll destroy her children'. It was not Jezebel's children who offended God, but the generational curse placed on Jezebel affected her offspring. When the king pharaoh refused to let Israel go, God inflicted plagues on the king pharaoh and his fellow Egyptians. God exterminated the firstborns of Egypt. It was King pharaoh who launched the rebellion, but God was exasperated against Egypt. Like blessings, the judgement of the Almighty God can be generational. That's why you need to remain careful with how you work with the Almighty God. Jesus wants to save you. He wants to save me. He wants to save the Church – His bride. Many love Jesus from the heart, but Jesus says, 'If ye love me, keep my commandments'.

The deception man received from Satan led to a divine separation between man and the Almighty God. And Satan is continuously wrestling to keep that God-man relationship broken. But Jesus came to fix it. Jesus died so that you can live. He was crucified because of you. The Almighty God allows Satan to operate because He's putting humanity to test. He wants to prove those who are like-minded with Satan. He wants to distinguish between the children of God and the children of Satan. In this end-time, Satan is employing so many strategies to keep you out of the Almighty God's domain. Satan can offer you the world. He carries out many of his activities in dreams. He comes with hidden strategies like sins of the mind. Beware of sins of the mind like unforgiveness and imaginary fornication. Unforgiveness is a hidden spiritual murderer. Cunningly, it kills your human spirit. It destroys your relationship with the Holy Spirit. Resentment is a silent killer – it can be suicidal. Fornication can destroy your soul. Be cautious of slandering – it's a camouflaged satanic sword. No matter the strength of your bond, slander can tear you apart. Sins are classified and have different effects on your physical existence on earth, but they all have identical eternal consequences – they have the strength to send you to hell. Any doctrine that supports sin is from Satan. So every Christian must have a desire to know the truth and abstain from iniquity. By that, the Holy Spirit walks you into perfection. Satan would never repent. His destiny is set. He has a specified period to operate. He's doomed – he's already condemned. But you can transform your will. You have a chance now and our Lord Jesus is ready to embrace you. The most terrible state you can be on earth is to live without the Holy Spirit. But when you submit your will to the will of the Almighty God, His will becomes your will and you would enjoy a healthy bonding with The Holy Spirit, which helps you truly understand the strategies of Satan. Missing heaven will be an eternal embarrassment. When Noah was instructed by the Almighty God to build the Ark, in preparation for the flood, many people only realized the truth when it started raining – Genesis 6:5 – Genesis 7. When Jesus was upon the mount of Olives, His disciples came to Him and asked, 'Tell us, when shall these things be? And what shall be the sign of thy coming, and of the end of the world?' Jesus replied, 'Take heed that no man deceive you. For many shall come in my name, saying, I am Christ; and shall deceive many. And ye shall hear of wars and rumours of wars: see that ye be not troubled: for all these things must come to pass, but the end is not yet. For nation shall rise against nation, and kingdom against kingdom: and there shall be famines, and pestilences, and earthquakes, in diverse places. All these are the beginning of sorrows' - Matthew 24: 3-8. Truly, we're living in the end-time. But exactly when this generation would pass away, remains a secret of the Trinity. However, Jesus further says His gospel shall be preached in all the world and then shall the end come - Matthew 24: 14. Jesus wants every country, every state, every city, every town, to hear the truth before His arrival. He wants every man to have an opportunity to be saved. He's revealing His truth to man because He loves man. And you would be without an excuse because you'll have to be judged. But Jesus preaches His gospel not because He wants to judge you, but because He wants to save you. When you reject His offer, you face His judgment. Jesus hates no man. Jesus hates Satan. But when any man decides to make Satan his everlasting master, Jesus hates him with the same passion He hates Satan. So, as you're beginning to see the signs of the beginning of the end of the world, you need to understand the strategies of Satan and remain glued to our Lord Jesus. Many dark angels are unleashed onto earth. Many satanic agents have been ordained in this world. When I was wrapping up this manuscript, I had a dream. I was in the midst of an assembly. I saw many people – some I knew, some I did not know. At some point, the Lord opened my spiritual eyes and when I looked at the people, I could see their heads transform into snakes. After a while, I saw them as normal humans, but whenever the Lord opened my spiritual eyes, I could see their heads transform into snakes. At a point, they realized I recognised their true satanic identity. Then, some of them attacked and started wrestling with me. It was difficult fighting with them, as the attack was intense. During the spiritual tussling, I heard people say 'they're fighting against him' and overheard someone say 'they will not overcome him'. I tried shouting the name of Jesus, but they couldn't let me open my mouth. I started saying the name of Jesus in my heart and eventually, I was able to shout the name of Jesus orally and repel them. Suddenly, I woke up singing, 'How excellent is your name, oh Lord, how excellent is your name, oh Lord, how excellent is your name, how excellent is your name, how excellent is your name, oh Lord, how excellent is your name, how excellent is your name, how excellent is your name, oh Lord'. The name of Jesus is our major weapon against satanic forces. Revelation 3 says the coming of the Lord would be as 'a thief cometh in the night'. Jesus can appear in a day of your least expectation. So, 'Be sober, be vigilant; because your adversary the devil, as a roaring lion, walketh about, seeking whom he may devour' - 1 Peter 5:8. Satan aims to help send as many humans to hell, as he could. Even the very elect can be captured – Matthew 24:24. But the Almighty God always speaks to His people. He always reveals information to protect His creation. He loves us!

Some time ago, I was on my way home, about 10:00 pm. I was living at the Juba Hill region in Freetown, Sierra Leone, with my wife and two kid-daughters. As I was moving around the Lumley Roundabout, which intersects the beach route, a retailer of recorded compact discs was chasing me, asking me to buy some of his CDs. I was driving and didn't want to get distracted and obstruct the traffic flow, but he kept bothering me. I then requested to see some of his CDs, but the ones he presented were worldly CDs —songs that glorified Satan. I then asked for Christian songs, which he tried getting out, but the traffic was moving and I drove off. A few minutes later, I found a safe parking position. When I got out of the vehicle, I couldn't find the guy. But I just had an urge in my spirit to get some Christian music CDs. I started searching around and found a video/audio compact disc shop, where I was able to get two Christian worship song CDs. Immediately I arrived home, I tried them and they were truly inspiring —great songs that glorify our Lord Jesus. And when I went to bed, I inserted one of the CDs. My inner man was touched until overwhelmed by sleep. In bed, I saw myself standing in a house. And suddenly, I heard a voice saying, 'Look at a horse coming', and through the window, I could see a horse descending. The horse appeared very tiny, as it was very far above. I looked away from the horse and after a while, I heard a voice say again, 'Look'. I looked through the window again and saw the same white horse standing, but this time, it appeared very mighty, even taller than the relatively high building I was standing in. Then right on top of the horse, I saw a man with humanly unexplainable features. His presence was spiritually captivating and I could sense overflowing heavenly anointing all over. With the help of the Holy Spirit, I then recognised the man on the horse as the Son of man, the Son of God, The Bread of life, the Living Water, the Word, the Light of the world, the great 'I AM', the Way, the Truth, the Life, the Ancient of days, the Lion of the Tribe of Judah, the everlasting Father, the Alpha and Omega, without whom nothing was made that was made. Then, I heard voices saying, 'Jesus has come'. Suddenly, I realized myself in bed and immediately explained to my wife. Before this encounter, the Holy Spirit had advised me to do a series on Facebook titled 'Understanding the Strategies of Satan', which was delayed. But just after that encounter, the Holy Spirit inspired me to do the series, as humanity needs it urgently. Fifteen episodes were successfully done on Facebook. But He now inspires me to do it in detail through this book. Our Lord Jesus loves us so much. He wants to keep a healthy bond with us. That's why He's revealing the strategies of Satan.

Truth is not judgemental. Truth is not condemnation. Remember, Paul says, 'All scripture is given by inspiration of God, and is profitable for doctrine, for reproof, for correction, for instruction in righteousness: That the man of God may be perfect, thoroughly furnished unto all good works' −2 Timothy 3:16-17. Rebukes and corrections are elements of ministry. If you refuse to preach the truth, Jehovah would hold you accountable. The Holy Spirit is revealing the strategies of Satan because He wants to save you from everlasting torture. The Almighty God says, 'Be ye holy, for I AM holy'. He wants you to be perfect, even as He is perfect. **Understanding the Strategies of Satan** is a guide to help you elude the snares of Satan. But the Holy Spirit with you and in you, who inspired this heavenly revelation is your chief guide. When you have Him, He leads you into perfection. Always maintain Him and do not aggrieve His personality. Jesus loves you so much and wants to spend eternity with you. I know many people love Him too, but Jesus says, 'If ye love me, keep my commandments'.

Immorality destroys immortality. Join the end-time army now and help defeat the army of Satan. So that when our Lord Jesus comes to receive His bride, He would say to you, 'Well done, thou good and faithful servant'.

I Love You and God Bless you – in the Name of Jesus Christ

Addendum

Scriptural References

All scriptures are taken from the King James Version of the Bible

Other References

Physical Research on Halloween – Wikipedia

Research on the Kaaba Stone –Wikipedia

Definitions

Kaaba Stone – A cuboid-shaped black stone/structure in Mecca, Saudi Arabia, where Muslims from different parts of the world converge to worship.

Ngewor – The Mende word for God. Mende is the largest ethnic group in Sierra Leone

Drop-outs – People who partially complete a project/course they embark on, which was not their original intent.

Servant of God – A Christian Leader

True Prophet – A Servant of God

Phoney Prophet – This refers to a false prophet. He portrays himself as a servant of God, but is an agent of Satan.

Matured Christian – A Christian knowledgeable and well experienced in biblical principles and the application

Baby Christian – A Christian not well knowledgeable/experienced in biblical principles and the application

Weak Christian – A matured Christian that can yield to Satan when there's an intense satanic attack.

Stubborn Christian – A matured Christian that cannot bow to Satan, even amid demonic oppression of the highest form

Dark angels – These are demons. They're the fallen angels, who were kicked out of heaven with Satan.

Chief Dark angel – This refers to Satan.

The Invisible Currency – The Mark of the beast; 666

Other Book by the Author

Samuel's first book entitled **Life as a Student** was published on 14th November, 2019 by **Kingdom Publishers**, based in London, United Kingdom. **Life as a Student** is available at Kingdom Publishers, Amazon and other renowned International Online Book Stores in different languages around the world.

About Divine Global Domain

Divine Global Domain is a writing ministry established to transmit the gospel of Jesus Christ. The major goal is to see mankind succeed on this planet and remain Indigenes of God's kingdom. We're focused on helping souls born into the kingdom of the Almighty God via books, songs, articles and movies, as inspired by the Holy Spirit. Also, we write on different issues affecting humanity, but in a Christian context. Divine Global Domain shall also engage in direct training, as we carry out our writing assignments. The training shall include ecclesiastical teachings and electrical-engineering related courses.

Social Media Contribution

Samuel does articles on Facebook and transmits inspiring messages on WhatsApp. He does minor commentaries on Twitter and Instagram, as well.

His addresses include:

Facebook @ Samuel Koroma

WhatsApp @ 23277861755

Twitter @ samneriah01

Instagram @ Samuel.koroma.16

Please follow me and together, we'll make this journey fruitful.

The Need for Christian Membership

To help you get a deeper understanding of Christian principles, you need to be a member of a local church – a church overseen by a pastor. Join a church that believes in the Trinity. Find a ministry that believes in the operations of the Holy Spirit and become a member of the Christian family. You need spiritual maturity to carry out your assignment and maintain your salvation.

The Cry for Mercy (Say this Prayer)

Lord Jesus, whatever way I've hurt you, whichever way I've sinned against you, where ever I've offended Lord, I'm sorry. Erase my sinful past and embrace me with your loving arms. Shower me with your unending grace and eternal mercy. Father in heaven, anything in my body, anything in my soul, anything in my spirit that disqualifies me from heaven, take out now – in the name of Jesus.